DARE TO DEFY

Dare to Defy

Challenging Stereotypes
and Looking at
Relationships in a
Christian Context

KENNETH W. CHALKER

The Upper Room
Nashville, Tennessee

Dare to Defy

The scripture quotations are from *The New English Bible,* © The Delegates of the Oxford University Press and the Syndics of the Cambridge University Press 1961 and 1970, and are reprinted by permission.

The stanza quoted from "Rise Up, O Men of God" is used by permission of *The Presbyterian Outlook.*

Book design by Nancy Johnstone

First printing: January 1981 (6)

Library of Congress Catalog Card No: 80–54478

ISBN 0–8358–0418–6

Printed in the United States of America

This book is dedicated

to *Wayne Calvin Chalker*,
      living still;

to *Charles and Vernita Nail*,
      parents and wonderful friends;

to *Grace Elaine*,
      who shares my life;

to *Laura and Wayne*
      who incarnate the word *joy*;

to *the people of Lexington Church of the Cross*,
      hearers and doers of the Word;

and

to *my senior high school English teacher*
      who, years ago, told me
      I would flunk out of college.

✍ Contents

Roles Miscast

Feelings Unowned

Conclusion

ᒥ Foreword

by James S. Thomas

In a time when confusion over moral standards has reached epidemic proportions, it is gratifying to read the good news of the gospel with great clarity. In an age when the drama of some religious expressions is too easily substituted for substance and when feeling in religion often excuses far too much, all Christians can be grateful for a writer who combines both substance and feeling in one book.

Without the self-conscious attempt to prove it so, Kenneth Chalker has given us a book that is soundly biblical. The words of Jesus, the illustrations coming from both the Old and New Testaments, the clear insights into such major themes as forgiveness, authority, despair, and rebellion—all of these are here.

This is a book that leads us through some of the most distressing and poignant real-life experiences that people can have to the redemptive word of biblical faith. From being typical to uniquely valuable in God's faith; from broken dreams to a new vision of life; from modern idol worship to the Master's gift of liberation—this is the journey that the author invites us to take.

Those of us who know Kenneth and Grace Chalker know them to be young but mature shepherds. Their ministry shows many of the fruits of faith that Mr. Chalker preaches about so effectively. The loyalty of a grateful congregation has good foundation. With a sound family life, the writer reveals a perspective on Christian family without once overlooking the perils that can—and often do—attend any marriage.

Finally, one is grateful for good writing. These are days when good writing—even the writing of letters—is left to the professional on the one hand, or the popular writer of easily marketed books on the other. In any case, good clear prose, expressing profound ideas and emotions from a Christian perspective, can never again be taken for granted. The writer of this book has given us all a good example: avoidance of involved theological language, with no loss of substance; descriptions of poignant human situations, without becoming maudlin or vague; visions of the good news in human life, without overlooking the terrible reality of human sin.

Kenneth Chalker's book is written for a wide spectrum of age group interest. Young people can find deep meaning in the author's understanding of the complex age in which they must grow up. And I found myself, as a father and church official, both inspired and judged by these chapters which I read at one time and with constant interest.

Canton, Ohio
December 16, 1980

∽ Introduction

Along Interstate 71 in Ohio there is a restaurant which caters to truckers. The menu is printed in a kind of "truck-driver-ese" with one section of diet selections listed under the bold question, "Is your rig overloaded?"

For many persons the answer to this question is a resounding yes! We are an overloaded people, too many of us overloaded with physical weight but more of us overloaded with emotional and psychological burdens which sometimes seriously cripple our "rigs." This book takes a look at some of these encumbrances and attempts to offer some heavy duty shock absorbers so that we might bear our loads rather than break down under them.

In the pages which follow, I have included many "word pictures" which portray persons and life events as I have come to see them. I share these pictures in the hope that they will be heavy-duty shock absorbers for whatever heavy loads the reader may carry. The value in doing this is that these portrayals, if nothing else, will convince those who read them that the burdens of life are common ones: it gives a person strength to know that what he or she may be feeling has been felt before.

Since coming to the pastorate I have learned a great deal about people—our joys, sorrows, needs, and fears. In all this I have discovered what is probably too obvious to note—namely, that most often the things which overload us are those burdens which we have taken upon ourselves or which we have allowed to be piled upon us without ever examining the load to see if the freight is worth hauling! Much of the time we carry burdens and agendas which are heavy—not because those burdens themselves are substantial, but because *we believe them to be* crushing, inalterable, and confining.

Thus, these "word pictures" are presented so that we might "dare to defy" the weight of many of the burdens we carry. We can do this by defying easy social stereotypes and debilitating role expectations. We can do this by defying the idea that feelings are best dealt with by being ignored or repressed. We can do this by affirming that Christian faith, rooted in the biblical witness, gives us now and always has given men and women the courage to defy those forces which often incapacitate us.

The Old and New Testaments are marvelous writings, for they contain the stories of ordinary men and women who, in the midst of life's ambiguity, made an extraordinary response in faith to God! Therefore the key to understanding ourselves, to shattering easy social stereotypes, and to defying superficial role assignments is to be found first in the lives of men and women who came to understand themselves and then shattered and defied those disabling forces long ago.

It is unfortunate that the Bible has been viewed by some as such an unreasonable book of unsympathetic judgment, and by others as a boring book about irrelevant, ancient people clothed in bathrobes and sandals! These notions are both seriously mistaken. The Bible is a real book about real people who faced the human dilemmas of faithlessness, fear, anxiety, boredom, meaninglessness, and confusion. Their stories are remembered because in the midst of all those things these people experienced God and defied the stereotypes and easy assumptions of their age. In daring to defy, they were moved to affirm what was true, hopeful, and good.

Obviously this book is not a definitive effort. It is instead a brief collection of some of the word pictures that have meant a great deal to those who first heard them. I hope what is presented will be helpful within its limited scope and will become more broadly applicable by encouraging the reader to dare to defy those particular stereotypes which he or she may face.

The title of this book, an exciting one to me, was suggested by Charla Honea and Linda Henson of The Upper Room staff after they had carefully read my manuscript. I am happy that the title, which I feel is dynamic, was generated by the material presented here. I am hopeful that each reader will find that title appropriate after reading the pages which follow.

Certainly one of the most crippling stereotypes of our time is the one which classes the church as a conglomeration of hypocrites and self-righteous bigots who are only interested in cramming for their earthly finals and heavenly reward. If these pages can help the reader defy that image of "typical Christians" and present something of the electrifying wonder of Jesus Christ, then this humble effort will have been useful indeed.

Kenneth W. Chalker
Lexington, Kentucky
December 3, 1980

SOCIAL
STEREOTYPES

✒ 1
Typical Christians

True maturity is our ability to be comfortable with people who are not like us. Persons from different backgrounds, experiences, nationalities, philosophies, social preferences, and religious persuasions need to be made aware of the need to appreciate one another's unique character. We all need to discover those situations in our own individual communities which might hinder understanding, goodwill, and mutual concern.

Let us suppose that you received a phone call from your mayor asking you to be the chairperson of a commission designed to seek out those structures in your local community which hinder the expressions of goodwill and mutual concern. As chairperson of that task force, where would you begin your work? Which situations in your community would you point to as needing to be interpreted or used effectively so that goodwill and mutual understanding might be promoted? Where would you focus your attention?

Would you take a look at the senior high school and say, "Well, what we really need to do is work with those kids! Those senior high young people are always in the way. They're always making a mess of something and getting out of line. We need to begin with our young people"?

Or would you point to the police department and say that we need to be more effective in communicating what the police are about?

Or in response to community problems such as low water pressure and broken water lines, would you throw up your hands and say, "What we really need to do is have a study that focuses on the functioning of the village council, and to make sure that the people in our community know what's going on"? Where would you place your efforts for promoting brotherhood and sisterhood?

If I were asked to be the chairperson of such a task force, I would concentrate my efforts on widening the respective applications of the word *typical*. In my judgment, contemporary usage of the word *typical* blocks our understanding of each other because often it is used to describe negative characteristics and associations.

Consider some of the unfortunate ways that you and I use the word *typical*. One of the phrases that we often hear is "typical teenager." Someone will look at an individual young person and say, "Aw, he's nothing but a typical teenager." Such usage of *typical* implies that this particular teenager represents a group of teenagers who are thought to be irresponsible or rebellious. Once we use the word *typical* to define an individual that is a young person, that young person can be nothing else in our minds than a troublemaker.

Another phrase that we use is "typical cop." What we mean by that is a person who is in love with the uniform, the gold or silver badge, who likes to flash a gun, write tickets, and harass teenagers—"typical cop."

The unfortunate thing about all such uses of the word *typical* is that once we call a person typical we steal that person's identity. We take that person's name away, and we replace it with an image of what we think it means to be typical in regard to who that person is or what that person does. We absorb the name, and we substitute for it an unfavorable image. This is frightening to me because it is very easy to hate and distrust a "typical teenager." It's not so easy to hate a specific young person we may know. We can resent the actions of a "typical cop" much more easily than we can resent the actions of a particular policeman who is also our neighbor and who happens to earn a living by enforcing the law. Once we put the word *typical* on someone, causing that individual to lose identity, we become indifferent to that person as an individual.

Consider your friends, neighbors, acquaintances. Are any of them typical? Probably not. As we come to know individuals, we see them as unique, special, and loved by God.

The word *typical* causes many hurt feelings and many sad situations. Eleven years ago now my wife, then single, had the opportunity and, I think, distinct privilege of being Miss

Ohio. Often there are phrases exchanged carelessly identifying "typical beauty queens" as brainless women with all appearance and no depth, all surface and no deep commitment, or as one comedian says, "all froth and no beer." All through that year Grace had to contend with images and phrases such as "typical beauty queen." On one occasion she was invited to make a speech before a group of young people at a university. Her appearance there was scheduled during the time that the campuses were recovering from the Kent State crisis and the Vietnam War involvement. At that time institutions such as beauty pageants were looked upon with great skepticism. The word *typical* was frequently used. As Grace drove onto the campus, a group of students was waiting there to welcome a "typical beauty queen." They had rotten eggs, tomatoes, and a barrage of signs. They egged her car and harrassed her as she drove down the street because she was typical. No one ever bothered to get to know her as a person. What a tremendous error they made in calling my wife typical.

One of the ways that we might get a handle on goodwill, mutual concern, and respect is to learn to use the word *typical* more appropriately. I believe we can begin to accomplish this task by listening to some very important words from Paul's first letter to Timothy.

Here are words you may trust, words that merit full acceptance: "Christ Jesus came into the world to save sinners"; and among them I stand first. But I was mercifully dealt with for this very purpose, that Jesus Christ might find in me the first occasion for displaying all his patience, and that I might

be typical of all who were in future to have faith in him and
gain eternal life (1:15-17).

In these verses Paul subtly and explicitly teaches us a key
lesson in getting along with each other.

First, he teaches that not one of us—whether he or she is
a patrolman, a preacher, a physician, a nurse, a business
person, or a homemaker—not one of us is free from error.
Not one of us is free from making mistakes in judgment.
And second, Paul teaches that for each of those persons who
ask, who realize that he or she makes mistakes in judgment
and has enough guts to say so, God finds an opportunity for
displaying all his patience. But the most startling thing of all
is that Paul says, "God has done all these things to show me
that I am typical of all who have faith in him."

Paul is saying to us very explicitly that before we label
another person a "typical cop" or a "typical preacher" or a
"typical something or other" and categorize that person's
personality, we must first remember to say, "I am typical of
all persons, because I make mistakes and I need displays of
God's great patience."

You see, if we can say, "I am typical," rather than,
"You are typical," we change our perspective, raise our
sights, and have a whole new set of standards for what
"typical" is. Instead of saying such things as, "Well, she's
just a typical parent," we might say, "I am typical, and my
children's ideas of what it means to be a parent are shaped
by my enactment of that role. I am typical, and the only
model that my children have is me."

Or instead of saying, "Well, he's just a typical preacher," about others in my profession, I have to say first of all, "I am typical," with the full knowledge that many people who judge what preachers are about will make that judgment on what they see in me. Saying "I am typical" changes my attitudes and remarks of disparagement.

All this means that each of us, in seeing ourselves as typical, begins to realize the importance of the impression we make. Nowhere is this more true than in our calling as Christians. Today we often hear, "Aw, she's just a typical Christian." Often that phrase is used to denote a nominal churchgoer who says pious things on the one hand and does completely different sorts of things on the other. We might see a person who in the name of Christ is always complaining about the rise in pornography, the increased sale of alcoholic beverages, smoking, and swearing, but who will support a war, cutthroat capitalism, and the established way of doing things.

I think that is a bunch of hogwash. I do not know any such Christians. I have never met a "typical Christian." Christian persons are those who are caught up in the dynamics of their faith, who live their faith powerfully and with deep consideration for the actions they take, and who have a great enthusiasm for caring and a great tenderness of love in their hearts.

What is typical is never any more or any less than our individual representation of what we believe. What is typical is never anything more than the impression that you and I make and the model that we give.

Therefore, it is my hope that in our dealings with each other as a community of citizens and also as Christian persons, we come to know and be strong enough to say, ''I am typical. God make me worthy of the great task that being typical presents.''

2

The Subtle Tyranny of Who and What

Several months ago I had an appointment with an architect whose offices are located in a downtown office building. The lobby of that office building serves as an entrance for the architectural firm and other businesses in the building. But also, early in the morning during the school year, that foyer becomes an *ad hoc* waiting room for elementary students as they wait for the school bus.

On this particular morning several months ago, it was cold and wet outside, so the foyer was being especially well-used by the elementary school students. As I walked through them to reach the stairway, I detected that they were having a very heated discussion among themselves on the value of being literate in society. They were talking about whether or not school was important. Most were angry that they had to go to school, and others were frightened because some "old witch" was going to give them a test. They made many other comments that one ought not to repeat, but that one is always astonished to hear from such young mouths. Their conversation intrigued me. I climbed halfway up the stairs and stood behind the wall, so that without being seen I could listen to more of it.

I had assumed that all the kids were agreed on their dislike for school. One little boy, however, mustered some courage and said, "Well, I think that social studies is a wonderful subject and I like it." (He didn't say wonderful, but words to that effect.) The response from all of the others was immediate and frightening. You would have thought that the boy had committed a great crime. The other kids began screaming, "Dummy," "Stupid," and "Idiot," until one voice was heard above the rest saying, "You're a freaky nobody! Nobody cares what you think!" After that, the only sound in that foyer was the sobbing of the little boy who liked social studies. He had just experienced the tyranny of *who* and *what*. That little boy suffered from the blatant tyranny of being attacked because of who people thought he was. When the other children called him "Dummy," "Stupid," or "Idiot," they came to think of him as "a dummy whose opinion didn't matter."

Now all of us know that children can be terribly cruel. But, I think that in growing up much of the thoughtless name-calling gets put aside, and we become persons of better manners, a bit more considerate than we were when we were in elementary school. But for some reason the great tyranny of *who* and *what* stays with us. Somehow, who a person is thought to be and what we assume that makes that person still inflicts great hurt, both emotionally and psychologically. The hurt inflicted is not as blatant as it was in that foyer two months ago when children were overtly cruel to the boy, but in adult life the hurt is still present and, if anything, more powerful because the tyranny of who and what becomes more subtle.

We have all known and experienced groups in which we have felt that we were not welcome. People have not said, "You're not welcome," but because of who we were thought to be and what that somehow made us become, we could *feel* the message loud and clear.

Nearly three years ago, for instance, a man told me that when he was buying his home, the real estate agent suggested to him that there were certain neighborhoods in the community in which he ought not buy. The suggestion was made because the agent felt that this individual would not be accepted in certain neighborhoods. Income, skin color, education had nothing to do with it. Rather, it was the subtle tyranny of *who* and *what* that real estate agent thought that person was.

There is a very special and tender story told in the Gospel of Luke:

One of the Pharisees invited [Jesus] to eat with him; he went to the Pharisee's house and took his place at table. A woman who was living an immoral life in the town had learned that Jesus was at table in the Pharisee's house and had brought oil of myrrh in a small flask. She took her place behind him, by his feet, weeping. His feet were wetted with her tears and she wiped them with her hair, kissing them and anointing them with the myrrh. When his host the Pharisee saw this he said to himself, "If this fellow were a real prophet, he would know who this woman is that touches him, and what sort of woman she is, a sinner" (7:36-39).

The subtle tyranny of who and what pervades the Pharisee's thought. He says, "If this Jesus really was a prophet, he'd know who that woman is and what she is."

Imagine the scene. Jesus is at the home of a prominent Pharisee—a leader of the temple community, a very righteous man, and probably a very wonderful fellow. He invites Jesus to dinner because Jesus is a holy man of great reputation. The Pharisee believes it will be a great honor to have this Jesus in his home.

In those days, when one went to a home for dinner, one did not eat as we do with our feet under a table sitting upright in a chair. The custom was to recline on either a couch or cushions with one's legs stretched out to the side of the table. Here is Jesus at dinner in a prominent home and in comes a prostitute. Everyone recognizes immediately who and what she is. She takes a seat, for reasons that are not altogether clear, by Jesus' feet, begins to cry, and then caresses and kisses his feet.

Well, the respectable folks are appalled, angry, but mostly embarrassed. They are reacting as you and I would if, while we were having dinner in our homes for someone we wanted to impress, a person from the community of notorious reputation came in and began to make overtures to our honored guest.

The Pharisee and his friends are not unlike us. You can imagine them covering their heads and saying, ''Doesn't Jesus know who this woman is and what she is?'' They all probably buried their heads in the pillows of the couch and tried to think of a way to get rid of her.

Jesus senses the embarrassment of the people in that home over this woman. He tells his host a parable. The parable is used to make the point that in no way does Jesus condone the life-style of this woman, but also that who and what she is in no way denies her access to God's love. Then the thing that astonishes and angers the guests the most is that Jesus, referring to the woman of notoriety in the community, dressed as a prostitute so that people would know what she does, says, ''This woman, because of her capacity to love, as misdirected as it might be, still lives a better life than those who choose those whom they accept by who and what they think they are.'' Such love, Jesus implies, is better than caring for people only on the criteria of who we think they are and what they represent. Can you imagine what that must have done to those folks? Well, they would have felt like throwing a pillow at Jesus! And one day the pillows became nails and a cross because of that kind of message.

Jesus eloquently states and demonstrates that caring and accepting persons defeat the subtle tyranny of *who* and *what*. He gives us the means to do this by imparting what I call the principle of *receptive affection*. This means that he takes people as they are and then, most astonishingly of all, finds a way to appreciate people the way they are as a beginning point to motivate them to be different. He does not just tolerate them; he finds a way to like each person he encounters. I feel Jesus sees in each one of us something that he likes and then is free enough in his own sense of personal knowledge of who and what he is to tell us what he likes about us. That takes a lot of courage.

There can be no greater need among people today than to feel the receptive affection of another person. We need it because the subtle tyranny of *who* and *what* in this country often makes us feel cold. Each of us is a victim of that subtle tyranny which classifies us by who we are thought to be and what it is assumed that makes us.

I know of a young man who, seven years ago, graduated from seminary with a textbook understanding and knowledge of counseling theory and skills. When he had been in his new parish three weeks, a middle-aged woman called him on the phone. She indicated that she needed to see him because she was having great difficulty adjusting to her life-style as a divorced person and that the change in income level as a result of the divorce was something that was causing great trouble in her home. Through the subsequent session that took place in the minister's study, the minister listened to this woman articulate her thoughts. He thought to himself, "What can I say? What can I do? What can I give to help this person deal with the problems she is facing and give her the strength to overcome them?"

After some discussion, getting in touch with the source of her pain, that woman that day taught this young preacher one of his greatest lessons. She said with tears streaming down her cheeks, "I don't need your advice, I don't need your help, and I don't need your material support. All I need to know is that somebody likes me."

That's all that any of us need—to know that someone likes us. For that receptive affection breaks the subtle tyranny of who and what and replaces it with a sense that we are somebody, someone, amounting to something.

✍ 3
Making the Entrance—
Missing the Cue

When he [Jesus] came in sight of the city [Jerusalem], he wept over it and said, "If only you had known, on this great day, the way that leads to peace! But no; it is hidden from your sight. For a time will come upon you, when your enemies will set up siege-works against you; they will encircle you and hem you in at every point; they will bring you to the ground, you and your children within your walls, and not leave you one stone standing on another, because you did not recognize God's moment when it came" (Luke 19:41-44).

The date was September 7, 1937. The air in Nuremberg, Germany, was filled with an electric excitement and an anticipation beyond all expression. People all through the city were milling around in a spirit of expectant enthusiasm waiting for the arrival of a special person. Preparations in

Nuremberg had gone on for months, and finally all things were ready. In the great square called Zeppelinfeld, a huge, sixty-foot iron eagle had been erected behind the speaker's podium. One hundred sixty thousand troops from the Labor Service Department of Nazi Germany filed into Zeppelinfeld in perfect rows and stood at attention for hours waiting for the special arrival. Thousands of Wehrmacht, Luftewaffe, S.A. and S.S. troops stood alongside with uniforms neatly pressed and insignias gleaming in the afternoon sun. Sixty thousand civilians lined the main road in Nuremberg. Thousands more were beginning to filter into Zeppelinfeld in anticipation of what was going to take place.

Finally, after hours of waiting in that charged atmosphere of anticipation and excitement, a dull roar began to rise from the crowd at the far end of the road. As people turned toward the sound, they, too, began to cheer. Coming through the center of the street was a lone Mercedes-Benz car. Standing in the back of that Mercedes-Benz was a man with his arm outstretched and a Walther 7.65 caliber pistol strapped to his side. As he rode through the street people shouted and cheered. "Sieg heils" were heard all over the city. Heels clicked and jackboots reverberated on the cobblestone streets. There was endless cheering and singing of the "Horst Wessel Song" as Adolf Hitler made a triumphal entry into Nuremberg.

It was late August, 1944. Liberated Paris, France, was experiencing the same atmosphere of electric excitement and enthusiasm. For days people had been hearing that a special person was coming. They all wanted to go out and see him. Now in the afternoon sun, with the excitement building among the thousands of people standing four and five deep along the Champs-Elysées, they watched for the entrance of a special man. As they stood there, each one hoped to get a glimpse of the special liberator who had released them from the years of Nazi tyranny. Finally, a cheer began to rise from the thousands of people gathered around the Arc de Triomphe, or the Tomb of the Unknown Soldier. Soon everyone could see him! There marching along through the center of the street was General Charles de Gaulle. The people cheered and threw papers in front of him expressing their utmost enthusiasm for his leadership and kingly nature.

One can think of many triumphal entries in history, particularly in the last forty years of this century. Such entries have been spectacular events filled with all the spectacle and drama of a Cecil B. De Mille film. We can remember these great spectacles as the world's leaders, good and bad, have entered our lives demanding and receiving our cheers and accolades and as they have traveled over streets covered with ticker tape instead of palm branches.

One can think of many examples. One might remember, for instance, Westminster Abbey nearly thirty years ago when the bishops of the church, the Archbishop of Canterbury, along with all the lords and ladies, gathered in that great edifice and stood at rapt attention as a young woman marched down the center of the aisle to be made queen of all England. What an entrance that was.

Or one might remember just a few years ago, when thousands of people massed into St. Peter's Square in Rome and cheered as a white column of smoke rose from the Basilica letting the people know that a new Pope had been elected. There was a new successor to St. Peter himself. Several days later, borne on the shoulders of the faithful, Pope John Paul II made his entrance through millions of cheering people.

Each of these entrances has one thing in common. *The one who was expected to come, came.* And he came in all his resplendent glory. The individual who possessed the quality that we wanted to cheer and shout about came forward from our midst and gave us what we wanted to hear. He gave the right cues upon his entrance. He had the right speeches with the right words, the words we wanted and were willing to hear.

Isn't it interesting, though, that today most of those great entrances are forgotten? Most people do not remember what a day it was in 1944 when Charles de Gaulle walked down the Champs-Elysées. And in their place, in place of all of these entrances, I find it amazing that each year on Palm Sunday people worldwide join in places of worship to remember together a triumphal entry that was made almost 2,000 years ago by an unassuming man who rode a colt through the cheering masses of people who called him their king.

In many ways his entrance was no different than those that I have just mentioned. People had waited expectantly for him for hours. They had heard stories about his incredible ability to change the lives of people. There was excitement and electric anticipation in the air as they waited to catch a glimpse of the man reported to be savior, liberator, and messiah. Thousands of people in the center of the capital city stood ready with a reception due a king.

But the uniqueness of Jesus' entrance into Jerusalem was that he was not what people expected at all, and he did not, according to society at least, give the right cues. People were all set to respond, to muster an army, to go to his side, and to fight with him as he liberated them from Rome. They were all set to respond to Jesus, but Jesus did not give the right speech! People were obliterated by it, hurt, and frightened. Remember, they were welcoming him as king of their nation; but as they gathered around him, he stopped on the outskirts of Jerusalem, looked over the city which was the symbol of their national pride, and said, "There will come a day when not one stone will be left on another in this city because you have not recognized the meaning of my visitation" (author's paraphrase of Luke 19:44). Can you imagine that? Can you imagine any king starting his rule over a country, or his leadership, by saying that the war is already lost? Can you imagine Charles de Gaulle or Adolf Hitler standing before those masses of people and saying, "I'm giving up! The war is over"?

Jesus' entry into Jerusalem was a staged event filled with all the world's pomp and circumstance to convey to us all that many of our entrances in this world are, in relation to the overall and ultimate purpose of God, of little consequence. Our own experience ought to tell us this. Think about all the flamboyant entrances we have made in our pasts that once seemed so important but now mean very little.

One might immediately remember one's own high school days. I can remember plotting the entrances that I would make into the school. There was a time when I would not have dreamed of darkening the door of my high school without wearing the right kind of white socks.

I remember that one of my sisters refused to step outside the house and make any kind of entrance at all unless her teased hairdo had been sufficiently lacquered with hair spray. She would not have dreamed of going anywhere without looking like there was a big ball of cotton candy on her head.

And I remember so well the dances, particularly the junior and senior proms, when my date and I would plot very carefully the moment of our arrival. We wanted to make sure that we never got there too early, always late enough so that when we walked through that door the appropriate entrance could be made. Then all of those things seemed so important, so crucial to our lives, and now they have nothing to do with anything at all.

One can remember that it was a lot of fun but our cues were all wrong. Our lines were designed to comply with what we were told was "in," "with it," "cool," "neat," or "sharp." No one wanted to be "gross" or "out of it." And as I remember, in the day-to-day struggle to be "in," all that we really did was make a lot of people and ourselves feel pretty much "out of it" most of the time.

The desire to make entrances and to be "cool" does not disappear as one grows older. All of us desire to make those kinds of entrances. Entrances are a part of life. Only the stages change. But many of our clamorings for entrances today reflect the inappropriate cues we have gathered from adult life.

Entrances, I believe, are designed to make impressions and impressions are very important. But the impressions we make with our entrances lose their authenticity and uniqueness if the impression we seek to make is designed only to ingratiate ourselves by responding to what society says we ought to be. We must make our entrances and impressions based on who Christ affirms that we already are—persons of worth who are loved; persons who are treasured regardless of style, appearance, or station. What the boss thinks of us, or what the bishop thinks of me, is important, and the impression we make on those people is essential; but my worth and your worth is more than the boss's or the bishop's opinion. And what the kids think of you at school is important, and the impression you make on your fellow classmates is important, but your identity is not restricted to their definition.

Jesus tells us that we witnessed his entrance but missed his cues. We did so because we were limited to what we thought we wanted. We had our own lines in mind. Already on that day in Jerusalem people had in their own minds what they wanted Jesus to say, and because he did not say it, they missed what he really said.

Think of all the persons who seek to enter our lives and

make impressions on them in our world. Often these people are responding only to what is considered "with it." They demand our attention, and they compete for our cheers.

I believe that ultimately the kings and queens of our time, whether they are kings and queens in the entertainment field or politics or whatever, as well as each of us, will have little effect or impact on the ultimate character of humankind if our lives are predictable cues for expected responses. Forty years from now, how many of us in this world will clamor to see the entrances of today's Hollywood starlets in bathing suits? They won't make any difference! Yet forty years from now, I can promise you, people will still remember when a man entered Jerusalem, riding on a colt while people put palm branches before him. And it will still give people courage and still express to persons the meaning of life.

Many years ago, William Shakespeare wrote a marvelous play entitled *As You Like It*. In that play, the character Jaques makes an eloquent statement:

> All the world's a stage,
> And all the men and women merely players:
> They have their exits and their entrances;
> And one man in his time plays many parts.

As we play our various parts and as we make our various entrances on the stage of life, we must remember that our greatest role requires our central identity. That great role must take to heart a man, William P. Merrill, who told how wonderful it was to be a servant in his hymn "Rise Up, O Men of God."

Rise up, O men of God!
Have done with lesser things;
Give heart and mind and soul and strength
To serve the King of kings.

FALSE GODS

ᕫ 4
Winning the Battle,
Losing the War

Have you ever known someone who was "annoyingly right" most of the time? Most of us have encountered such a person, who seems to be able to shoot our carefully planned argument or point of view to pieces with just one sentence or a few words that convey a fact that we have never even thought about before.

We all have encountered the individual who seems to have the opinion that proves to be right over the long haul. We know from experience when such people make a comment that they have been right before, so we become rather afraid to offer our own point of view. We think, "Now that person's generally right, so he's probably right again, or she's probably right again. I won't say what I think because I'm probably wrong—again."

Most of us can tolerate people who are usually right because they are wrong a sufficient amount of the time to keep them humble. But some people who enjoy being right most of the time are also obnoxious about it! The Old Testament character Elijah is a good example of the kind of person to whom I am referring.

Nine centuries before the birth of Christ, Elijah was a great prophet in Israel. First and Second Kings tell what he was about and what he did. He was one of those persons who was always right in what he said.

During part of Elijah's life, the great king Ahab ruled in the part of Israel called Samaria. Everything was going well with Ahab until he got married. From there on his life started to go downhill. The problem was that Ahab believed in the one God of Israel, the God that the Old Testament refers to as Yahweh. But his wife Jezebel believed in another religion in which the god's name was Baal. Now everything would have been fine except that Jezebel wanted Ahab to go to church with her! Elijah had a fit! He began getting messages from God that since Samaria was now ruled by Ahab who went to the wrong church, punishment was on the way. Elijah made a great prophecy to Ahab in front of the people on a festival day, saying that a great drought would befall the land. Ahab was so angry at Elijah that he banished him from the kingdom. Elijah went to live along a river where he was fed by ravens. Elijah had to hide because he was unpopularly right again. A drought did occur. Years later Elijah predicted that the drought was going to end. Coming out of hiding, he went to Ahab and told him, "It's not going to end unless you let me do what I think God is asking me to do." Ahab had no choice. So

Elijah in his righteousness called for a great contest. It is recorded in chapter 18 of First Kings.

Elijah said, ''All right, all you folks who believe in Baal, I'm going to prove to you once and for all that I am right.'' And so he challenged all the priests of Baal to a contest. Elijah said, ''I'll meet you tomorrow on the top of Mt. Carmel. We'll set up two altars. We'll cut up a bull and put the pieces on both altars. Then, we'll each call to our god. The god that shoots down fire and consumes the offering will prove that he is the one true God'' (author's paraphrase, verses 21-24).

Elijah was pretty egotistical because he did not challenge just a couple of priests; he challenged 450 of them. And so the next day the people assembled at the base of Mt. Carmel to watch Elijah and the priests of Baal go up to the top and build their altars. They cut the bull and laid it in pieces on the altars. Then the prophets of Baal started to do their dance and go through their religious practices to call their god to come and consume with fire the offering that was prepared for him. The priests danced from the beginning of the morning till mid-afternoon. They danced and they sang and they whipped themselves into a frenzy calling, ''Baal, Baal, come and deliver us from this challenge.'' Nothing happened.

Elijah believed that he was right, so during the time all those priests were dancing and singing and asking Baal to come down and consume the offering, Elijah would stand off to the side shouting his taunts: ''What's the matter? Did your god take the day off? Maybe he's sleeping this after-

noon? Maybe he can't hear you? Yell a little bit louder!''
(author's paraphrase, verse 27).

Pretty soon all the priests of Baal lay down exhausted
around the altar. They gave up, and Elijah said, "Now, my
friends, I'm right again, but let me make the contest a little
bit harder. This way you're really going to be convinced."
He dug a trench around the altar and threw in all kinds of
grain offerings. Then he ordered that great casks of water be
brought and poured all over the wooden altar. The water
flowed down and filled the trenches. Then Elijah said,
"And now, Lord God, come and consume this offering." A
flash of fire came down from heaven and consumed the
altar; the water evaporated. Nothing was left. The people
were astounded! They stood at the base of the mountain and
shouted, "Yes, Elijah, you are right again. Yahweh is the
real God. We will worship him."

But Elijah was not content with just being right. He was
riding high on a victory. The battle had been won, and with
victory in his heart he did an incredible thing. Elijah took
the 450 priests (who, regardless of their error, were people
who believed sincerely in what they were doing), with the
help of some of those who now thought that he was always
right, down to a valley called Kishon and slaughtered all
450 of them. Elijah had won the battle, but because of his
actions he had lost the war! People were incensed by the
manner in which he was right, and the very next chapter in
First Kings tells how the people rose up against Elijah for
his actions against the prophets of Baal.

Today there are still people who worship Baal; the name

has changed, but they worship him all the same. There are disciples of various spiritual leaders, there are those who believe in the power of pyramids, and there are those who believe in all kinds of cults. They are all led by misdirected people who are just plain wrong. But the worst thing that we could possibly do is persecute such individuals for their error. And there are those who, in response to being right, take the ones who are wrong to their own respective valleys of Kishon. Instead of being content with being right, such individuals take the "wrong" person and "slaughter" him.

There are many examples. Let's look at a marriage for a minute. Let's suppose that the wife in the marriage has become involved with someone outside the marriage relationship. After a time that affair is discovered by the husband. Now, the wife who has become involved in the extramarital relationship is wrong, whatever the reasons (and there might be very good ones). All kinds of things might be going on in her life which would make that act understandable, but it's still wrong. The husband is justifiably shattered and hurt, feeling betrayed and feeling that his life is broken. But let's suppose that those two persons in this marriage relationship decide that they will not split, but stay together. The wife repents and is honestly sorry. All of a sudden the marriage takes a different direction, because both partners communicate and realize some things that were missing in their marriage. But let's also suppose that afterwards, the husband reminds the wife every time an argument comes up of what she did. The husband never lets the wife forget that he remembers what once happened. He holds it over her like a club; for the sake of being right and winning a point, he destroys the marriage.

Or how about in our businesses? A manager may know that an employee has made a mistake. Then, forever after the mistake has been made, the manager never again trusts responsibility to the employee and never lets him or her out from underneath the thumb.

Or how about our attitude as Christians in respect to our role in the church? We can be right in our devotion and our dedication, but wrong in how we apply it.

Once I was at a retreat, and after I had spoken one morning, an ex-lay leader came up to me and said, "I need to talk to you." So we made an appointment, and he began to tell me about his life. He said, "You know, I was involved in my church. I loved it dearly. I contributed heavily to it—my time, my talent, *and* my treasure. I worked hard. I was a church school teacher. I was involved in the leadership positions. I was diligent in putting programs across. But I got sick of going to administrative board meetings and council on ministries meetings and sitting there with people who didn't come to church, who didn't really care as much as I did, who didn't give, who didn't work, who didn't do anything, but had the same vote as I did! I got so angry that when I sat in church with them I couldn't even stay there. So I quit." All his work, as right as it may have been, was spiritually self-righteous because of the way he applied it. He won his point but he lost his love. He was not a source of inspiration to the people, but a vessel of resentment.

If one isn't careful, being right can lead to resentment toward others. It really can, in the church or anywhere else. It is hard not to become angry with people who expect quality church school education for their children, yet refuse to teach. It is difficult not to be irritated with those who feel that, because they teach five days a week professionally, they are able to withhold their trained skills for forty minutes one Sunday a month. It is easy to become disappointed when people refuse to accept leadership or fail to see a commitment through. But as right or as justified as that point of view may be at times, we cannot be like Elijah and opt for Kishon and "slaughter" people with whom we disagree. Regardless of our respective levels of commitment, we must care about each other. The responsibility of being right means that we must also love those who are wrong and admit that many times we are wrong.

Let me illustrate: Linda was fifteen years old in the early 1970s. She was pretty, intelligent, but not very popular. She was considered by most of the people in her hometown to be a hippie, often seen in the crowd that used drugs. Her parents were committed people, involved in the life of their community, who had given their children many things—including love. They were justly concerned about Linda's attitudes. She was becoming cynical and had started using bad language.

Despite Linda's protestations, her parents insisted that she go to church with them. Sunday after Sunday she would come, and in the classrooms of the church school would say to people, "You don't know what this Jesus is about. He was the first great dropout, and the church today has no understanding of what he is about.''

The youth counselor in the church saw Linda as his special project. He had his work cut out for him. At youth meetings she was often disruptive; on one weekend retreat she smuggled marijuana in her sleeping bag and was caught smoking it outside her cabin.

The youth group had planned a trip to the mountains during the summer. Linda had arranged with her boyfriend to meet her at the campground. He followed the youth group, an hour behind, in his own van.

Just before lights out at the campsite, Linda asked the counselor if she could go to the restroom. Later, after a three-hour search, he found Linda with her boyfriend in the back of the van.

In the next hour the counselor was right in most of what he said to her and to her boyfriend. He was right when he said that she had betrayed his trust. He was right when he said that she had broken a moral code. He was right when he said that she had broken a great personal code, and that she had thoughtlessly used the whole group for her own ends. He was right in all those things.

But then he became righteous, and he called the other young people. He stood Linda up in front of them and rebuked her. He challenged her life-style and said that Satan ruled it, and that she was against God and that God was therefore against her. He was so convinced that he was right that he publicly admonished her in front of a group.

A week later the news was everywhere. The tragedy was,

however, that Linda's parents were destroyed by the righteousness of other well-meaning parents who looked at Linda and thought that her parents had somehow gone wrong. And Linda? She was obliterated. Because not only was the counselor right, but he took her to the valley of the Kishon and he slaughtered her there. Her reputation, her credibility, her self-esteem were ruined.

The counselor thought he was right. But I believe that Jesus would never have sentenced Linda to that Kishon. The counselor was right, but the counselor was also very, very wrong. His self-righteousness only increased the suffering of Linda and her parents.

Are you right about things? Rejoice that you are. But in the final analysis that is only part of the great issue. We need to be right. But it is not so much the correctness that is important, but the manner in which we love and care for those who are wrong.

5 ✍

A Human Being or a Utility Closet?

In the theater or in films or in television productions, there is a term that is often used called "typecasting." Typecasting refers to a situation in which the person playing a role is cast in that role because, without much acting or using much makeup or changing his or her voice, that person just *is* the character he or she depicts. The film roles that have become legendary, or the television programs that have remained popular even in reruns, are often those in which the main characters have been, or at least seem to have been, typecast. Several come to mind.

The first would be Clark Gable. He appears to have been typecast as Rhett Butler in *Gone with the Wind*. He did not act much in that movie. He *was* Rhett Butler. At least it seemed so. We remember that film, in part, because his character fit so well.

Or, how about Spencer Tracy? One of my favorite films as a younger person was *Boy's Town*. Spencer Tracy was a great Father Flanagan. He was typecast in the role, and we remember his portrayal of the priest because of it.

What about Marilyn Monroe? She was certainly typecast, and victimized by that typecasting, as innocent but seductive in *The Seven Year Itch* and *Some Like It Hot*.

Or, how about George Cleveland? Do you remember George Cleveland? George Cleveland played "Gramps" in the original "Lassie" series. When he died, "Lassie" was never the same because George Cleveland, "Gramps," was gone.

Katherine Hepburn was typecast as the independent-minded yet feminine character throughout her career from *Adam's Rib* to *Rooster Cogburn*.

More recently, Ron Howard has had difficulty breaking out of his typecast mold as a freckle-faced, red-haired imp, seen in "Mayberry R.F.D." and "Happy Days."

Or, another example, would be Robert Young in "Father Knows Best," who, for several years, captivated the nation with an image of a father that fit.

If I were to typecast a movie of the New Testament, and specifically the life of Jesus, there is one role which I think almost any career person in this congregation, including the preacher, could play. We could be typecast in the role I have in mind and be convincing in it.

The role that I think most of us this day could easily fit would be the part of that great Roman himself, that notorious character of the New Testament, Pontius Pilate. We could fit that role, you and I, very well, because we are a lot like him.

Let me tell you a little bit about Pontius Pilate. Pilate was a competent, extremely confident, well-trained Roman bureaucrat. He knew what he was about. All his life he had worked hard, pushed hard, prepared well, and remained loyal, so that at forty-five years of age he had been chosen by the Roman emperor as someone exceptional. The emperor appointed him to be provincial governor for Judea. Pontius Pilate was a nice guy; you would have liked him. He was well-mannered, rich, and sophisticated. He appreciated good music, good books, and great plays. But, having achieved his lifetime goal, he was now, at least as the Gospels portray him, a bewildered man. Life at the top was not as he thought it was going to be.

Pilate became skeptical; at one point in the Gospel of John, Jesus said, "I am the truth. That's who you have in front of you." Pontius was skeptical because his life had seen so many twists; he looked at Jesus and said, "Jesus, what is truth? Is there anything that is ultimately true?" (author's paraphrase of John 18:37-38).

Pilate drank too much. He found out that at the age of forty-five, in order for him to talk with friends and to become uninhibited so that he could enjoy himself or feel free in talking about his own life, he first had to have a few belts before he could warm up. The problem kept getting worse.

At forty-five, Pilate remembered all his achievements. He looked at his great robes and his seal of office, as he stood on what was called "the pavement" and gave judgment to the people. Pontius remembered all these things and felt miserable. He decided that somewhere along the ladder of his success he had lost his humanity. No longer was he seen as a human being, but more as a utility closet, chock-full of marketable skills that were paid for by people who wished to use him.

Well, what happened to Pilate? How are we like him? Listen to him under pressure and you will see.

Once more Pilate came out and said to the Jews, "Here's this Jesus. I'm bringing him out to let you know that I can find no case against him. I'm going to set him free." And Jesus came out wearing a crown of thorns. His head was bloody, as well as the purple cloak that the soldiers had used to mock him and make him look silly. "Behold this man," said Pilate. The chief priests and their henchmen were standing in the crowd, and they saw him and they shouted, "Crucify him, crucify him!" And Pontius looked out and said, "take him out and kill him yourselves! For my part I find no case against him." And the Jews answered, "Pontius, we have a law. You're forgetting our law says that any man who calls himself the Son of God should die. If you don't enforce that law, Caesar will be mad and you might lose your job, Pontius." When Pontius heard that, he was more afraid than ever. Taking Jesus back to his headquarters he asked Jesus, "Where have you come from?" But Jesus gave him no answer and Pontius said, "Do you refuse to speak to me? Don't you know who I am? I have the authority to set you free and I have the authority to condemn you to death. Why don't you speak to me?" Jesus looked at Pontius and said,

"The only authority you have comes from on high. God gave it to you" (author's paraphrase of John 19:4-11).

There was Pilate, in turmoil. The crowd was screaming for him to do something he did not want to do. Pilate was caught up in all kinds of relativistic business ethics and in the idea of what it meant to be an executive. He knew the Jews were right when they said if the emperor heard, the emperor would be mad. And he asked Jesus, "Why don't you speak to me? Don't you realize the authority I have?" And right there Jesus cut through forty-five years of that man's experience and went right to his basic problem with one sentence. Jesus said, "The problem with you, Pilate, is that you have never realized that you have no authority at all. The only power you have is what God has given you. You function only to the limits that he allows."

Well, this is the reason I think that many of us could play the part of Pontius Pilate. Because at the base of what you and I do, most of us believe what he believed. We believe, like Pilate, that we hold the reins and that we are in control. We believe that we drive the horse—that we have our acts together. We believe, like Pilate, that we are in control of our lives, that we have authority. Some of us are like Pilate because we believe that we have received from this life what we have duly earned by our own sweat and initiative.

And some of us, like Pilate, believe that a mature person is strong, never revealing tears, always showing a stiff upper lip. We pretend to be self-assured, never admitting weakness or areas where we might need help. We are afraid to do that. We don't even talk about those things with our mates!

And we certainly believe, like Pilate, that the person of real maturity is not outwardly religious. We might ask, as Pilate did in his headquarters, "Jesus, where do you really come from? Give me the lowdown." But we do not talk that way in public.

What happens when we live by that silly code is that one day, like Pilate, we realize that instead of being a human being we are regarded as a utility closet by our company and ourselves. We look at our portfolio to see what skills we have acquired, and we value ourselves based on what is seen there. We rate our importance by how thick the portfolio is. In other words, we rate ourselves by the functions we perform.

I had lunch with a Pontius Pilate several months ago. He is likable, effective, and successful. He said to me, though, "Sometimes I do get twinges that it just isn't worth it." I asked him, "Well, what do you believe? What holds you together? What do you think about God, and what place does he have in your life?" And then my modern Pilate said, "I don't have that kind of need right now. I just don't need what others seem to get out of Christian faith. God exists, I suppose, but I'm just not into that. I've made my own way!" I remembered the Psalms and a hard lesson I learned, and I asked, "Don't you even have the need to say thank you?"

One year ago I was at a point in my life where I needed to be reminded about who was in control of my life. I had gotten to the point where I thought I was the prime mover in my life and in my work. One day when I tripped over a box that had been left in the hall because there was no room to put it anywhere else in the church, I vowed that I would build our addition by myself if I had to! I was convinced that I was the prime mover.

And then one morning after breakfast I discovered I could not move the right side of my face. I was scared. I thought I was having a stroke! I ran to the doctor (that's almost literally true), tripped into his office, and said, "Doc, you've gotta help me! You've got to fix my face and fix it by Sunday!" And he looked at me, shook his head, and said, "There's nothing I can do."

For three weeks the right side of my face would not move. When I took a drink, or when I ate, I was really embarrassed and self-conscious because I had to hold my lips shut so food would not come back out. I made a bigger mess at the table, I thought, than both my children together. When I went to sleep at night, Grace had to tape my eyelid shut because I could not close it. When I smiled, half of my face worked and the other half just sort of lay there. I looked as though I was sneering and angry at everybody. And I learned something in the six months it took me to move my face again. (And I was lucky because I was going to be able to move it again. Many people suffer worse diseases than Bell's palsy, and will never move their bodies again.) I learned that I was more than a function. I began to hear what Jesus told Pontius Pilate 2,000 years ago: "You have no authority at all. You function only to the limits that God allows.''

Anyone who truly believes that he or she is self-made and owes nothing to anyone else is suffering self-delusion. To rest self-worth totally in accomplishments and deeds is misdirected.

You think you are a crack salesperson? You know you have clients who buy from only you because you are good and because you know your business and your product? They tell you they won't buy from anyone else because no one else is as competent as you? Do you value yourself as a good salesperson because you are skilled, and think that is *all* you are? Well, what are you going to do tomorrow if an embolism stops the brain function that allows you to speak? What will you think of yourself then?

You think your ability has put you where you are, and that you have earned your comfortable income, your house, your car, and that you have done it yourself? What will you believe about life and your purpose if tomorrow, for reasons unknown, your retinas begin to detach and within three months you are totally blind? What will you think of yourself if all you've done is value yourself as a function?

My intention is not to scare you or to imply that God sends these things upon people purposely. But sometime we are going to have to stop committing the great sin of arrogance, the great sin of thinking that our values are in our skills that we alone develop.

You know, the wages of sin is death; the Bible clearly states that. We might think that is pretty archaic. But it is applicable today. The wages of sin is still death, and arrogance is a sin. The wages of that sin is death, and if you do not think so, you take a look at all the career people who think they have the reins in their hands, who think they run it all themselves. The pressure keeps building up, and everyday these arrogant people are dying from high blood pressure, heart attacks, strokes, and cirrhosis of the liver (since alcohol is the only thing that dulls their senses). Don't ever stop believing that the wages of sin is death; it is so not because God sends it upon us, but because we bring it upon ourselves. When are we going to let go of the reins and realize that God is in ultimate control, and that his love for us, not our function, gives us our value?

I feel God does not care whether we think we need God or not. God cares only that we love him enough to look at the facts of our lives, the abundance of our lives, and that we are grateful.

We must, in the privacy of our offices or of our homes, stand and, instead of looking straight ahead or to the side, look up, raise our hands, and say, "God, we are nothing without you. All that we have comes from you. We give you thanks."

We have no authority at all and no power at all! The only authority and power we do have is what God in his wisdom gives to us.

∿ 6
Our Salt Content

Can you imagine what it must have been like to hear Jesus speak? Can you imagine what it must have been like to stand on a hillside and listen to a man reported to be the Son of God speak to you about the meaning of life? Can you imagine what it would have been like to experience his enthusiasm and his overwhelmingly good sense of humor? Can you imagine the force of his sincerity and compassion for persons, often conveyed through the use of a phrase or a word that would change a person's outlook on life? Can you imagine the captivating character of his examples, drawn as they were from the everyday life experiences of those around him and enabling each person, regardless of the level of his or her education, to glean from him truths of inestimable value about God and human life? Can you imagine what it must have been like to hear that kind of man?

One of his most memorable, difficult, and yet most intriguing, sayings incorporates one of the most common elements of nature, an element common to us all—*salt*. Jesus takes salt, which is common to everyone's experience, and uses it to convey great meaning for those to whom he is speaking. "You are salt to the world. And if salt becomes tasteless, how is its saltness to be restored? It is now good for nothing but to be thrown away and trodden underfoot" (Matt. 5:13).

Rick was twenty-two years old, unemployed, untrained, undisciplined, and uninterested in being either trained or employed. He had been living at home idly since his graduation from high school, which itself had been "iffy" since he never applied himself. He was in trouble a good bit of the time. His parents did not know what to do with him. They had no rapport with him at all, but he knew how to use them. He was cruel to his mother, indifferent to his father, and manipulative of them both. He believed his parents owed him support, for as he said, he "didn't ask to be born!" He expected privacy, no restrictions, and no questions. He resented and rejected rules, believing that he ought not to be expected to follow anyone's guidelines but his own.

One day after he embarrassed his mother in front of her friends, she became so upset and hurt that the threshold of her tolerance was finally met. From within her the years of disappointment and anger burst forth as she shouted,

"Rick, you are a useless human being! You're not worth salt!''

Nancy was thirty-three, attractive, intelligent, articulate, and interesting. Her problem was that she didn't think that she was any of those things. Nancy and her husband were parents of three young children. She felt that he rarely saw them. Nancy settled the fights, washed the dirty faces and hands, and cleaned the house that the children cluttered. Her days, she felt, were exercises in nothing more than total futility, the low point being the scrubbing of the toilet bowl and the high point being the leaving of the house to shop at the grocery store (with the kids, of course).

One afternoon while Nancy was cleaning the basement closet she came across an old trunk; in it she found her old high school yearbook. Leafing through it, she turned to the activity section and came across the picture taken when she was head majorette and head twirler of the band the year they had been state champions. The band was the best in its class and she was the leader. Underneath her picture in the year book was the caption, "With pizzazz, looks, and personality—her future is in the stars." Sitting by that old trunk that day, she did not think so. Later that evening, after the children were in bed, and while her husband was mesmerized on the couch in front of the television, she went to her room and began to cry. She sobbed, "I feel useless! I'm not worth the salt in my tears."

John was a well-regarded young executive with five years' experience and a good future. Because his company was not doing well, he felt his job was in jeopardy. Thinking about how he might secure his position in the company and even obtain a promotion that might increase his job security, he went to work and spent twenty-four months researching and developing a new product line. He developed a marketing field and a whole strategy for how that market could be promoted and utilized for the sale of his new product. He had everything worked out to the smallest detail. Ready to present his ideas, John took in his briefs and promotion charts and laid them in front of his supervisors and the company marketing engineers. They rejected his proposal; three weeks later John was transferred three states away. Sitting at his desk he said, "Two years of my life have been wasted! I might as well have gone out and pounded salt!"

These are only three examples of many that could be given of persons who feel useless. We might think of persons who reach the age of forty and with that experience look out over their lives and say, "My major goals have been reached. What is there left to do? Where will I channel my life now?" Or we might be mindful of retired persons who think that the significant portion of their contribution to culture and people is over and are faced each day with a feeling of uselessness. Or one might think of junior high young persons who as early adolescents realize very acutely that they are considered too old to do some of the things they still like to do and too young to do many of the things that they wish they could do. They find themselves trapped in the middle and frustrated beyond belief because they just do not seem to fit. Or we might think of persons who often feel they are as useless as leftover vegetables. (That means not enough to amount to much and too much to throw away.) All of us, at times, feel useless; often those feelings come to us when we least expect them. We wake up one morning and look at the tasks before us and think, "How useless I am." Jesus addresses those of us who have such feelings of uselessness by saying, "You are the salt of the earth!" Then he asks the important and pertinent question, "In the moment when you lose your sense of value, your salt content, when you lose that, how will you regain it?" (author's paraphrase of Matt. 5:13).

In these verses Jesus is very much concerned about people who feel useless. His purpose for these words is to enable persons to acquire a taste for life that is seasoned with gaity, spontaneity, enthusiasm, and commitment. But he does not just leave us there. He gives us a handle on how to do that and offers, by implication I think, suggestions for how those of us who often feel useless might regain our saltness again.

One thing we must remember whenever we read the scripture, particularly those things said by Jesus, is that many times his comments were never fully recorded. Often just the main point was written and remembered. Thus, the context of his message has sometimes been lost to us. This verse about salt and regaining our sense of saltness, or our sense of value, is a case in point. Jesus makes the important statement, "If you lose your salt content, you'll be nothing more than that kind of salt we throw out into the road which is trampled underfoot by men." What does he mean by that? He is reflecting, I think, on the ovens in first century Palestine.

People in those days kept ovens outside their homes. Such ovens were brick. In order to keep heat in the ovens overnight so that there would be a cooking fire in the morning, people cut troughs in the bottoms of the ovens and laid in banks of salt. The salt acted as a catalyst, maintaining the heat level in the coals which were spread over the top of the salt. After the fire had burned down and was banked for the night, the salt underneath kept the heat. The next morning the oven temperature could be built up again quickly and easily. But after many weeks of use, the salt in the trough, subjected as it was to the constant heat of the oven and daily routine, would lose its ability to keep the heat. The salt lost its savor.

Jesus, therefore, was reflecting on a practice known to persons: when the salt failed, the oven had to be shut down, and the useless salt removed and thrown out. Therein lies the message of how *we* start to feel useless. So many of us lose our sense of saltiness, our sense of being able to contribute in meaningful ways, because, like the salt in the oven, we are often subjected to constant pressure and daily routine. If we never escape the routine, if we never do anything different, we lose our sense of value, as we have no chance to replenish ourselves. Like the salt then, we lose our effectiveness. Thus, we need to regain our sense of value, or salt, by reducing the temperature of our oven—our work, our home, or personal life.

In more easily understood language, I think Jesus is

saying, "Don't feel guilty if for two hours out of the week you need to go and play a set of tennis." Don't feel guilty about that. It contributes to your value so that when you're back at your tasks you do them better. Or he says, "Don't feel guilty if, when confronted with feelings of uselessness, you decide to chuck it all and walk in the woods for two hours to regain your salt. Don't feel guilty about that. Once the salt has lost its savor, of what value is it? You've got to replace it." He says, "Don't feel guilty if every once in awhile you have a craving to ride a fire truck, or take an extra hour out of your day to be with your family, or to be with yourself. Don't feel guilty if, when confronted with the tasks of your home and the demands of your kids, you get a babysitter and take off and spend the afternoon shopping or doing whatever helps you replenish yourself. Once the salt of your life has lost its savor, what value are you in your work?" He is saying to us, "Don't feel guilty if in response to a sense of uselessness you cut a couple of meetings and stay at home several nights in a row. Don't feel guilty if you forget the work that is piled up on your desk and spend a couple of moments or even a few hours talking with your spouse. Don't feel guilty if you need, once in a while, to sit in a totally quiet room." Jesus, I believe, is saying that anytime we do anything to reduce the stress that is produced by constant routine, we are engaged in meaningful work. Because if we do not do this periodically, we destroy our salt. Some people will say, "I never take a day off. I work all the time. My company demands it and I have to do it." And when persons say that to us, sometimes they say it in a self-righteous way, suggesting that anyone who *does* take some time off is somehow skirting his or her responsibility. But you know if you just keep plugging away at the routine, it will not be very long before you lose your value to everyone with whom you come in contact. You will only be doing things by rote, and the strength of your character and the salt of your personality will become lost.

Jesus' message is designed to overturn our sense of uselessness, not by changing the pressures, but by helping to change our attitudes as we face them.

Sometimes I begin to feel about as useless as a glass of water given to a drowning man. When I get that way, I try to discover places around me or things to do in order to regain my sense of salt. One of those places is not very far away. Sometimes when I feel pretty useless I take a drive out along a certain road. I stop down there just below the spillway by the bridge. I shut the car motor off and go out and sit on the hood. I look like an absolute fool. There I am, in my coat and tie, sitting on the hood of my car. If I sit there and pay attention, I will hear the water going over the spillway and rushing into the creek. I look across the dry reeds and into the woods there beside the road and see the evidence of new life in the emerging spring green. I get a new appreciation for the beauty of auburn, the richness of russet, and I hear the birds singing their individual songs in the trees. Soon I find myself surrounded by a symphony of sound and color. When I do that or things like that, it does not take long to regain my salt.

"You are the salt of the earth!" Shake loose from the

continuous routine and provide yourself with the spice of vitality, so that you might be richly seasoned in a world that manifests a creator who is full of wonder, flavor, and hope. "You are the salt of the earth!" Realize it, appreciate it, regain it, treasure it.

7

Strategy for a Fourth-Quarter America

There was a time, many years ago, when the Hebrew people were becoming very pessimistic about their future. They were tired, depressed, and feeling as though God had somehow abandoned them. They felt they were on a vicious treadmill going nowhere, but having to move very quickly just to stay in place. They became apathetic about what they were about as a people. They started asking questions like, "What good does it do to worship God? It never gets us anywhere. People who don't believe in him have as good a life as we do. What's the point of it all?" At the same time that these kinds of questions were being asked by a growing number of people, there arose in the land a prophet by the name of Malachi. Malachi said to himself, "Something must be done to lay claim on the imaginations of these people, to let them know that life is not as depressing and sullen as they think it is.'' And so, wherever he could get a hearing, Malachi stood before the crowd and said this word from the Lord:

> There will come a day unlike any you have seen. And when it comes it will be like a blazing furnace. And those of you who are now tired but who have had faith in God, you will feel a great soothing. And on that day you will break loose like calves from the stall! (author's paraphrase of Malachi 4:1-2).

Are you like the people in Malachi's day, or are you different? When your alarm clock goes off at 5:30 or 6:00 in the morning on Monday, do you jump right out of bed and do one hundred jumping jacks, twenty-five one-armed push-ups, sixteen deep knee bends, take twenty-five breaths of air, and then jog to the shower singing, ''Oh, what a beautiful morning?'' Is that you?

Or are you more like the people that Malachi knew? When your alarm goes off tomorrow morning, will you confuse the sound and answer the phone instead? And finally, when you come to your senses, will you hang the phone up, shut off the alarm, and then slither out of bed? Will you then stub your toe on the corner of the bed and stagger to the bathroom? Then as you stand in the shower with your toe bleeding, thinking about all the things you've got to do in the coming week, all the mundane and ragtag things, will you suddenly realize that you've forgotten to turn the water on? Is that more like you?

Lately, I've been meeting a lot of people who are

exhausted—spiritually and mentally—who, like the people in Malachi's day, are losing their faith in just about everything: in God, in their country, in their families, and in their work. As a result, they are becoming pretty cynical, and even apathetic, about it all. It seems that many of us are becoming a lot like a football team I used to know.

During my high school days we had, without question, the worst football team in the league. It was not the coach's fault, and it was not the players' fault—it was the fault of the band! The biggest guy on the line of scrimmage was five feet eleven inches tall and weighed 190 pounds soaking wet. But in the trombone section of the band the average height was six feet four inches and the average weight was 211 pounds. Those were just the girls! By the time the fourth quarter had rolled around in any given game, the fans had gone home. People were depressed. The guys on the bench and out on the playing field were disillusioned. The offense was demoralized. The defense was exhausted. All the plays had been made, there were not any more secrets the team could pull from the hat, and as they faced the final minutes of the fourth quarter, they knew the game was lost.

I think that today we feel a lot like that football team in the fourth quarter. It's no wonder that so many of us are tired and depressed a lot of the time, because we're making the plays of our life as Americans in the fourth quarter of the twentieth century. We have gone through three quarters that have been exhausting, draining our resources and our energies. And even though we may not have participated in the previous three quarters, the collective drain on us as American people and on our emotions affects us all. Let's review the game thus far, looking at the plays that have been made in the first three quarters of this century on behalf of the American team. We have had a pretty tough game. And now in the fourth quarter, we are running the patterns almost out of force of habit, rather than with any intention and enthusiasm.

When the whistle blew signaling the first quarter of this century, the Americans went on the field with our grandparents on the first-string team. They went out on the field with energy unsurpassed, and with the overwhelming conviction that there was not another team in the world league that could beat them. They believed they had limitless resources. They had been taught by leaders like Teddy Roosevelt from the time they were very young that the strategy for the American team was to charge. Our grandparents were making the plays with quarterbacks like Henry Ford, Thomas Edison, and Alexander Graham Bell. We were led through tough plays by coaches like Woodrow Wilson. Even when we had a couple of hard downs, like the First World War, we emerged from those downs and scored the point. The fans went wild and said, "Yes, this American team is number one."

But success went to our heads late in the first quarter. The government became corrupt from its top levels down; a postwar inflationary economy threw prices sky-high; we had organized crime at an unsurpassed level. Many fans and players began to be disillusioned at the end of the first quarter because the team was beginning to look a little shabby.

By the time the whistle blew and we started the second quarter, some of our parents were already taking their places on the line. As the replacements were made, the plays went on much as they had at the end of the first quarter. As a result, the whole team soon found itself in a depression. The only thing that saved our team in the second quarter was the fact that all the other teams in the world league suffered from depression, too. And so the world league teams got new coaches. Russia got Stalin. Germany got Hitler. Italy got Mussolini. The Japanese got Tojo. And all of those coaches told their teams that the only way to be number one was to obliterate all the other teams in the league. And our parents said, "No, we want a New Deal," and so we elected another Roosevelt as coach.

After the teams clashed on the global gridiron at the end of the second quarter, the whole world was bloody. We left the field a big mess with a lot of dead players behind.

During halftime, when we were back in the locker room, the assistant coaches took us to task. Assistant coach Joe McCarthy tried to "psych" us up to go out and battle the Communists. So when the second half opened up, we ran from the locker room and went right out on the field to meet the Korean team. We charged right out to do battle again.

Early in the third quarter many of our generation were starting to play. In the huddles we heard about how we were loosing yardage in a "space race," and so we all got concerned about scientific play. Scientific play was pushed hard. We studied hard, and we changed our whole game plan. As we changed our game plan, we had a coach that went right along with us. We had Kennedy for a coach and a quarterback named King, who called the plays in a brand new way. Some of the fans got so upset because the game was being played differently that they shot the coach and the quarterback.

So we got some back-to-basics coaches like Johnson who talked about a Great Society, and Nixon who said, "When the going gets tough, the tough get going." But by the end of the third quarter, we were so disillusioned and our team was so upset that nobody wanted to move.

So here we are, in the early minutes of the fourth quarter. Inflation is choking us; we have a distrust of leaders and institutions. We question so many people's motives. We are growing more selfish, and there is a general sense of emotional and mental exhaustion in the face of pressures. What is our game plan? What are we going to do?

Malachi has a suggestion: "Those of you who feel so tired, but have loved God, for you there is great soothing if you will take it. And because you are well fed from the food of faith in God, you shall run like calves from the stall!" (author's paraphrase of Malachi 4:2).

When I was in junior high school, I worked part-time on a dairy farm. One of the jobs the farmer gave me was to feed hay to the yearling calves that were kept in a large enclosed pen in the barn. After the calves had been fed, I would open the gate and let them run out into the pasture. And those calves that had been turned loose from the stall would run and kick and jump and seem to rejoice in being free.

One evening the barn was dark upstairs, and I wasn't paying a whole lot of attention to what I was doing and didn't even bother to turn on a light. Instead of throwing hay down to the calves, I threw straw. The farmer soon noticed that the calves were not eating and quickly realized the problem. He came upstairs as I was busy kicking down another bale of straw and said, "Ken, if you want to see the calves run, you've got to feed them right!"

It seems to me that the reason you and I do not run in this fourth quarter is that for three quarters we have not been fed right, and we are choosing not to be fed right now. We are a vitamin-deficient people trying to play a tremendously important game on junk food. We feed on straw instead of hay. The straw of television programming that passes itself for entertainment and absorbs our leisure does little to refresh us; the straw that says there is an income level to measure our success at work does little to nourish self-worth; the straw of political slogans which we are fed numbs us with its meaningless jibberish and does little to sustain a sense of community esteem; and material things, instead of allowing us to be free from chores, enslave us with a desire to want more and do little to satisfy deeper hungers.

None of those things can make us run in uninhibited joy. And none of them in and of itself can give us the zest for living that demonstrates that this life is important, exciting, and dynamic!

Malachi knew the answer; even today he teaches us in

this fourth-quarter America. He says to us as a team, "Are you tired, are you weary, are you languid, depressed, and worn? Maybe you're feeding on straw. Know this, God has made us all, and if we let him, he provides the bread that we need to energize our spirits, vitalize our bodies, and enable us to run."

ROLES MISCAST

∽ 8

I Remember Mama

Most of us have had a mother who has loved us and cared for us, and we would readily acknowledge the unique impact a mother has on the life of her child. Our mothers' effect on our lives can be measured in both our reactions against and our response to the kind of person she was or is. The lives of those few of us whose mothers cared little for us are as much affected by her presence as those of us who can remember her special comforting and love.

We could spend many hours thinking about how we feel about our mothers. The expressions we could give those feelings are endless.

To have the opportunity to make this kind of impact on the life of another person is a significant responsibility— especially in today's society. Today, women are reacting to the role of motherhood and its responsibilities in a variety of ways. Some women are finding they feel ambivalent about the role of motherhood as it has been traditionally portrayed. Many mothers in our culture feel as though they are inadequate, somewhat irrelevant to the "important" aspects of life. They feel they are involved in an often thankless and unglamorous role.

Never in the history of humankind has it been more difficult to be a mother. There have been many times in history when it has been *as* difficult as it is now, but never has there been an age or a cultural setting in which it has been *more* difficult to be a mother than it is today.

There was a time, for instance, during the European Renaissance, when motherhood was considered square, children thought to be nothing more than an encumbrance, and social systems created to get the children out of the parents' way. Homelife was thought to be archaic and not really the "in" thing.

A similar situation is in force today, and in response, fewer and fewer women are *intentional* about their motherhood as one of their primary roles. Almost all women accept it when it happens, but fewer and fewer are intentional about that role as a primary and noble function. The same could be said about fathers. Fewer and fewer of us are intentional fathers in terms of what fathering means as an ongoing process.

Being a mother can be terribly frustrating. Few of us truly enjoy doing laundry, wiping little bottoms and runny noses, cleaning up spills of chocolate milk and apple juice, or running to the grocery store. In addition, some mothers feel their influence on their children's lives is often less than visible. A mother can teach her child manners, vocabulary, and consideration; then, after letting her child spend one afternoon with the neighbor kids, or sending him off to one week of school, she might bet that the child who comes back bears no resemblance to the one who walked out. By the time the young person is in high school, I think many mothers today would be willing to believe that their child is an alien from another planet. Often it seems that nothing that a mother has done in the years that she has been with the children in the home has made any significant impact on them.

And if that were not enough, mothers today must compete in a society which is increasingly demanding that they fulfill a new role, that they be able to expound on economic theory and the inflationary spiral caused by OPEC oil prices. Say what you will, today's culture seems to value the "career woman" more than the "mother." And in such a world the question is asked, "What do mothers know?"

There was a time in ancient Israel when motherhood carried low status. The Israelites were without strong leadership, the cities were not safe, terrorism on national trade routes was high, the populace was fearful of social and moral collapse, and law enforcement officials, when they did exist, were suspected of corruption. People began to cry for a great warrior—some dynamic leader who would rise up, raise an army, and come to Israel's aid by setting things straight. People asked for a great man, a leader of people, a strong, mighty, masculine warrior. But whom did God send? Who saved Israel from destruction? Listen to these words from Judges:

> In the days of Shamgar of Beth-anath,
> in the days of Jael, caravans plied no longer;
> men who had followed the high roads
> went round by devious paths.
> Champions there were none,
> none left in Israel,
> until I, Deborah, arose,
> arose, a mother in Israel (5:6-7).

God did not send a great warrior to raise an army but one who was as a mother in Israel. Under Deborah's influence, the Hebrews became a great tribe of people because she had to give what no one else had to share. She gave her people the fundamental and ultimately significant aspect of motherhood which was and is *a sense of relationship*.

In an age that cried for power, Deborah became a center of affection. In a time that cried for security, she offered people encouragement. In a time demanding strong lines of racial segregation, she taught acceptance. In a country that called for law and order, she imparted and merited trust. In a civilization that sought status and reward, she inspired strong values in her people. And in an age that responded only to hate, she began to teach people to initiate acts which reflected the loving thing to do.

To do those kinds of things, God sent a mother to Israel; of all the important men and women of the age, she alone was remembered because of who she became: she became as a mother to her people.

The spring before my last term in seminary I served a church in rural North Carolina. At that time in our nation's history, we were struggling with the Watergate situation and the conflicts people had in relating to and supporting the federal government and national priorities. People on American college campuses, young people and others, were suggesting that the traditions like family, affection, and parenting were no longer important. One was instead to become involved in the really important issues.

In that parish, which was very small in terms of the size of the structure and the congregation, but large in boundaries, there were many gravel country roads. At the end of one of those country roads was a log cabin. The cabin was situated off that road in a stand of pine trees. Within that log cabin lived an old woman, her daughter, and son-in-law. The daughter and son-in-law, in the two years prior to my coming there and during the time I was there, had left their home in the suburb of a city nearby and moved out to that log cabin to be with the daughter's ailing mother. They had done so because in these last years of her life the mother was blind, deaf, and unable to speak. The only activity she had in her life was that the daughter and son-in-law would lift her out of her bed early in the morning and set her in a chair. Then at night they would lift her back into bed again.

I visited there on several occasions. In talking with the daughter, I came to realize a unique aspect of these persons' lives. The loving and caring that the mother had given to the daughter was now being returned to her in a special way. The daughter commented, "I want you to know that I am here because I remember Mama, and all that she was and is to me.'' Some might say the mother was inadequate or even irrelevant. But the daughter cherished her and continued to love her and care for her because their relationship was special.

Inadequate, irrelevant—yes, at times I suppose that being a mother is those things. But ultimately, what *greater* role and status can there be? What greater comfort, what greater strength, what greater sense of purpose in this life can there be than the uniquely special relationship between mother and child? The relationship that mothers share with their children is especially significant and perhaps more essential in today's world than ever before.

∽ 9
How Does It Feel to Be a Father?

One of the questions that is invariably asked of a husband after his wife gives birth to the long-awaited and expected child is, "What does it feel like to be a father?" Or, if it is the second or third child in the family, the question becomes, "What does it feel like to be a father, again?"

The answer to this question requires considerable thought. Unfortunately, when it is asked, usually one hour to three weeks after the birth of the baby, all fathers can do is give a rather stupid-looking grin and try to change the subject. It is a difficult question and one that fathers ought to be thinking about and answering all through their lives and the lives of their children. "What does it feel like to be a father?"

There is a great sense of pride in being a dad. I remember being in the delivery room during my daughter Laura's birth. In order to be there I had to don the hospital gown. I had the green surgical gown, plastic shoe coverings, and the little cap over my hair. I sat next to Grace as she did what she was supposed to do, being just as proud as could be that I was a new father. There is a great deal of excitement in being a father. Exhilaration. A euphoria that numbs you to everything else, and of course, there is a certain sense of fear.

I also remember the day that Grace and Laura were released from the hospital. I drove down to pick them up and went to the maternity ward. Before Laura was allowed to be released, the nurses wanted to make sure I knew how to bathe her. And so I had a class in baby bathing. The nurse was showing me how to hold her and how to work around the remaining portion of the umbilical cord. After everything was over and the nurse had Laura wrapped up, I called the nurse over to the side and said, "Babies are pretty tough, aren't they? I mean, they don't break real easy, do they?" There's a certain sense of fear in being a father.

In the course of being a parent, father or a mother, one feels such emotions—and many others—many times. There is one feeling, however, that seems to occur to fathers more often than to mothers. And often a father finds himself dealing with this emotion alone. That emotion is the feeling of being "detached" from his children.

The first time that feeling of detachment really hit me was also during that hospital experience. I went down for a feeding time, in which I was allowed to be in the hospital room with Laura and Grace. Laura was brought into the room, and I was given a bottle so that I could feed her. But as I looked at Laura and Grace there together, I realized how detached I was from that situation. There were my wife and child already enjoying a special binding relationship that made them so close. Laura and Grace had been together physically for nine months, and at that moment Grace already knew that little girl really well. Better than anyone else could know her. And as I stood there and looked at my daughter, I realized how much I did not know her. I realized how much of a stranger this little person we called Laura was to me at that moment.

It was at that moment that I learned one of the challenges of being a father. I learned that the tender closeness that seems to be naturally present between most mothers and their children is something fathers often find they must work very hard to develop with their children. Understanding the far-reaching implication of this statement can enable a couple to go a long way in understanding themselves, each other, and their parental task.

Being a father in contemporary America is no easy task, specifically because at many points it is a battle in overcoming the detachments associated with the traditional role of the male parent—detachments generated by the time and energy demands of a job. Social pressures in our country tend to define rather narrowly the cultural expectations of a father.

A father may feel he is expected to remain detached from the major development of his children. He feels he must be about the tasks of his company's business and the world's affairs, while the task of raising children on a day-to-day basis and being a major influence on their lives is often restricted to the mother. It's sad, because so many times fathers are the victims of many things around them that do not allow them to do what they feel they must. They get caught in a bind, and it's hard to reconcile the different pressures to succeed and still be devoted fathers.

Dr. Spock, for instance, that widely read pediatrician, indicates in his book on child care that women ought not to be alarmed, or even surprised, if their young children are frightened of their father. He says that women ought not to be alarmed about this, because sometimes infants and young children have not had the opportunity to be associated with a man whose voice is low, whose face is rough, since the fathers are not around that much. Clearly, Spock is implying that the detachment of a father is to be expected!

Today many husbands and fathers are unsure about their roles as fathers, just as their wives are confused about their roles as mothers. These rapidly changing roles and expectations have taken their toll in marital conflict. And what this means is that in this country there are more than twelve million children growing up in families where there is no father.

What I derive from that staggering statistic is that the role conflicts and conflicting expectations about each other on the part of husbands and wives has caused many men to abandon the role of being a father in the home altogether. In 90 percent of all divorces involving children, custody of those children is awarded to their mothers. This is a strong indicator that the detachment of many fathers from their children has long been recognized by society.

There are some things we can do to become more effective fathers in overcoming the detachment from our children.

The first and most important is that a father needs to let his family know that it hurts him to leave every morning. Fathers need to be honest about knowing all too well that another full day in the lives of their children is going by without their ever seeing a significant portion of it, often without their ever taking part in the first words that their babies say, or the first steps they take. There are so many firsts with children, whether they are young or older. A way to overcome missing these firsts, I think, is not to stay home, or to quit one's job and let one's wife go to work, or to change roles. One way to deal with the problem is simply to say that it really hurts, and to let your family know how much they mean to you, and how you would like to be with them even when you cannot.

One of the hardest things for me to do many mornings is to leave the house when Laura is sitting at the breakfast table with Cheerios smeared all over her face (she calls them O-E-O's), knowing full well that great events are going to take place and I won't be there. Kids need to know that you'd like to be with them, and they can understand that at a very young age.

Second, fathers need to ditch the idea that being successful and faithful to our work means that our families must always come second. The importance of holding as sacred special hours in the week, or one day with one's family, is essential not only to our effectiveness as fathers, but also to enhancing the quality of our work when we return to it.

Third, it is helpful for wives to point out positive contributions which their husbands make to the lives of their children. In many troubled marriages, the criticism I hear is generally directed toward the irresponsible attitudes of the father as enumerated by the wife. Many times this criticism is justified, especially for husbands who expect their homes to be their own personal castles in which they are to be kings. But on the other hand, conflicts arise in the home because husbands are riddled with criticism for what they do not do. And in many cases that is unfortunate. Many men go to the office and stay there, not because they are particularly in love with their work, but because it is the only place in this whole world where they feel any sense of success.

Fourth, fathers must free themselves from society's stereotypes. There are men who fear raising children, particularly sons, because they believe that they can't play football very well, or be aces in tennis, or be the strongest fathers on the block; because of these things, they feel that they do not make good fathers at all, and therefore tend not to try. But, you know, God never intended for fathers to be coaches. Our greatest asset is always the measure of our love.

And finally, fathers must learn to demonstrate the cohesiveness and strength of our families by the love that we show our wives. My children love for me to hold them, chase them around the house or the yard, take them for bike rides, swim with them, and wrestle with them on the floor. They laugh and giggle and run to meet me when I come home. But the greatest contribution I can make to their lives, to their sense of well-being and belonging, is to hold their mother and tell her that I love her.

10

And They All Say, "Give Me. . . ."

One day a little girl was waiting impatiently for her father to come home so that the family could have dinner. Finally in exasperation she said to her mother, "Mommy, if the stork brings our babies, if Santa Claus brings all of our presents, if the Lord gives us our daily bread, and Uncle Sam our social security, why do we keep Daddy around?"

It seems that in no age has there been more confusion about the function of a father. Everything from television programs like "One Day at a Time," where the father is absent and never missed, to the almost automatic procedure in our courts to award custody of the children to the mother in a divorce seems to imply that there are no really good answers to the question, "Why do we keep Daddy around?"

Being a father in American society is ambiguous at best. Fatherhood is a confusing role with many voices shouting blame at men for the fact that they do not do well at it, yet offering little guidance for how they might do better.

"Why do we keep Daddy around? What good is he anyway?" Nathan Scott is one father who would really like to know.

Nathan is a fairly successful man in his early forties. He and his wife are the parents of three children. All three of them are teenagers: Todd, who is thirteen; a sixteen-year-old son, Jim; and an eighteen-year-old daughter, Leslie, who will begin college in the fall. They live in a modern home along with a useless pet poodle that has a leaky bladder when she gets excited.

Nathan is an executive with an electronics firm. He has achieved a level of relative comfort and security for his family. He works hard at his job and has always done so. The week before Father's Day is no exception. At least six days a week, he is in the office by eight in the morning and is rarely home until after six at night. His wife, Barbara, and the three kids each lead very active and individual lives. Young Todd plays in the little league; Jim is caught up in television, cars, and the gang; and Leslie dates a great deal and is either in the bathroom fixing her hair or going out to a party, show, or concert.

Nathan, for some reason, has been thinking during this past week about his role as a father. He is confused and a little frightened because he doesn't really feel that he is a part of his family. On the Friday before Father's Day, he leaves his office and arrives home. This is the scene that he encounters.

Leslie's boyfriend, John, has parked his car in the middle of the driveway, so Nathan has to put his car along the curb in the street. Upon entering the house through the family room, he encounters his son Jim sprawled out on the reclining chair with a soft drink in one hand and a sandwich in the other, watching "The Early Show." Nathan speaks to his son, "Hi, Jim." Jim, without moving his eyes from the television set or turning around to see his father, raises the hand with the sandwich in it and mumbles a greeting.

Nathan then walks into the kitchen, and as he goes past the refrigerator, a streak of lightning named Todd crashes past him. Todd is dressed in his baseball uniform. He greets his father by saying, "Dad, I need some money for after the game. Can you give me a couple bucks?" Nathan, handing Todd three dollars, says, "Where's your mother?" And Todd responds, "I don't know. Can you give me a ride to the ballfield?"

Walking into the living room, Nathan finds Leslie's boyfriend, John, sitting on the couch reading the paper. Nathan speaks to the young man buried behind newsprint. Without standing up, without putting the paper down, without making so much as a motion, John mumbles from behind the newspaper, "Hello, Mr. Scott." Moments later, Leslie descends the staircase. She sees her father and says, "Daddy, John and I are going to a movie. Can you give me five dollars?" As Nathan hands her the money, Jim walks in from the family room (there is a commercial on television, so he, too, takes a break) and says, "Dad, can you give me the car tonight?"

Nodding that he thought it was OK, Nathan hears a shriek from the basement, "Nathan, I'm in the laundry room; can you come down and give me a hand? The washing machine's plugged up!"

One hour later while eating a cold, clammy, chicken salad sandwich all by himself at the counter in the kitchen as his wife gets ready to play bridge, he finds a card with "To Dad" written on the envelope. At that moment his wife walks into the kitchen and says, "Oh, that's your Father's Day card from the kids. They're not going to be here Sunday morning; they've all got plans, so I thought you might like to read it now."

A most unusual thing then happens. Nathan, a forty-three-year-old successful person, begins to cry. His wife, for a moment, thinks it is probably just the sentiment, but then through his tears she hears him say, *"All they say is give me."*

You know there are probably many things that can and ought to be said about Nathan and his family. Like a lot of fathers, he has never thought about the meaning of his role until just recently. When he does, he feels sorry for himself. Nathan finds that when he starts to think of his role as a father, he determines that the only one who is ever glad to see him is the little poodle that jumps up and down when he walks in the door and then wets on his shoe.

You could rightfully say that somewhere along the line Nathan got into the habit of seeing his role as the provider and measuring his effectiveness as a father by how well he performed that function. Always responding to the "give me" demands, he somewhere lost sight of his more crucial role: not just to give what was requested, but to establish the relationships along the way so that he is permitted in and is able to help his children come to understand what they need.

You know, responding to "give me" is not a new role for fathers. The Bible indicates that the role has been around a long time. Isaac lay dying, a sick, blind, old man, and Jacob whispered in his ear, "Father, give me your power."

The daughter of the wealthy Caleb is another example. Her story is told in the book of Joshua. Caleb was a great land owner. As a wedding gift, he gave his daughter a great deal of land. And yet, on that day when she could have said so many wonderful things to her father, she took the only opportunity she had to speak to him and said, "Would you give me some wells, too?"

David lay dying and his two sons (he had a lot, but two of them) were battling between themselves about who ought to be the ruler. So each son in his own way, in the last minutes with his father, went to him and said, "Will you give me your kingdom?"

And Jesus tells the story, the unforgettable one, about the prodigal son in the Gospel of Luke. The prodigal son says to his father, "Will you give me what is rightfully mine?"

In each instance the father gave what was asked to his child. Each father was faithful to the duty he felt of responding to the loud "give me" that he had heard all his life. And you know, each one of them, as far as we know, died without a word of appreciation, a goodbye kiss or a hug, and without a tear from his child. Isaac, Caleb, David, and that brave man from the Gospel of Luke who welcomes back the prodigal, and many another father, died successful but alone.

Let's go back to Nathan for a minute. As he cried over his chicken salad sandwich he felt that he had failed with his children, and he began to think that as soon as they could fend for themselves he would no longer be in a position to give. Therefore, his children would not have much to do with him. It scared him. So he did what a lot of fathers do at that moment; he blamed his job for the time demands that it placed upon him. He blamed himself for never making his children enough of a priority, and he blamed his wife for not teaching them to respect him more. Now the realization of some errors can be helpful, but the sad thing is that none of those things will help Nathan.

I honestly believe that fathers would do much better at fathering and at being husbands if their children and their wives would be sensitive enough to express more appreciation than they so often do.

Fathers need, more than ever before, to examine their roles and make some changes. Spouses, and particularly children, are going to have to learn to show some degree of appreciation for what fathers and husbands are about and what they do, in fact, accomplish. Sometimes the *only* place a father is without honor is in his own home. Everywhere else people appreciate him, but never there, where it would mean the most.

Being a provider is a difficult task. There are always pressures to provide more or better. The economic conditions of our society demand it just to stay even.

And there is also the responsibility to relate closely with one's children, and most especially with one's spouse. But that is really hard for a man to do if he feels that none of his efforts ever make an impression.

On the other hand, there are fathers who work too much and whose work has become an obsession, not something they enjoy. There are fathers who do not spend enough time with their children. There are fathers who really do not know what their children think, like, or do. There are fathers who spend more time on the ball fields, the tennis courts, and the golf courses than is healthy for their family life. And there are some fathers who treat their wives pretty poorly.

But there are no fathers, and no mothers, who should be treated like Nathan Scott. No one deserves to be ignored and used.

FEELINGS
UNOWNED

11

Pressure—Life on the Pipeline

Dear God, right now I feel like a worm, not a person.
I feel so used by other people. And to make it worse, I
  feel resented by the very same people who use me!
Sometimes when my back is turned, I can feel everyone
  making faces at me, sneering in derision.
O God, stick close to me—I'm up to my neck in problems
  and all alone.
I feel like the walls are closing in around me. And in the
  dark I can see starving lions ready to swallow me up
  and digest me into oblivion.
My strength drains away like water, and my bones feel
  loose and shaky.
My heart feels like a lump of hot, sticky wax melting
  inside my chest.
My mouth is as dry as a broken piece of clay pot, and my
  tongue sticks to my jaw; I feel trampled and beaten.

Do you ever feel like the individual who wrote these words? Do you ever feel like you are being "digested into oblivion?" The individual who wrote these words could have been a frustrated homemaker or perhaps a bored retired person. These thoughts could have been written by a teenager feeling on the outside of the in group or by a man or woman whose job was in jeopardy. These words could have been written by a doctor, a minister, a business executive, a factory worker, an FBI agent, a union leader, a politician, or a teacher. These feelings could have been expressed by nearly anyone under pressure. But in fact, these are the feelings expressed by the great King David, who expresses them in the twenty-second Psalm. Although the thoughts have been paraphrased by me, they belong to David—a David under pressure.

Pressure is something all of us experience at one time or another. We all know what it feels like. We have come to know it well in modern life. To a point, it is necessary. It is a part of everyday living to be under a certain amount of pressure to accomplish things and to begin work on others. But lately it seems that more and more of us are experiencing destructive amounts of pressure which threaten to cause our collapse.

Today the pressure seems to be sustained over longer periods of time. We often feel as though we are coming apart. More and more we find ourselves strained by long hours of difficult work. Our family members are running in many different directions. Continuity, purpose, and direction seem to be fading from our lives, as we try vainly to meet the increasing demands upon us.

This is the point at which the pressure gets dangerous. As sustained as it often is, we begin to think we are disintegrating. This is why we need to have the emotional seams to handle such pressure. Too often we do not. We might do well to handle pressure by discerning the important difference between a pipe and a reservoir.

Consider a pipe, used to convey water from one place to another. It performs this function by immediately sending on the water introduced at one end by delivering it to the other. When pressure is applied to the water within the pipe, larger quantities can be conveyed through the pipe because the water moves more rapidly. Although the volume which can be moved increases under pressure, the diameter of the pipe never changes. When the limits are reached under pressure, the pipe explodes. The pressure is released, but the pipe is destroyed.

Unlike a pipe, a reservoir collects water and grows deeper as a result of the various sources from which it draws. It can only give what it has collected and stored. Because of this, reservoirs are by their very nature *resources*. They contribute from their fullness and handle the pressure of nature's severest storms.

Life in American society is too often geared to make us be effective pipes. We are encouraged to cope with this nuclear age by taking all the new data to which we are introduced and delivering it effectively into our daily lives. We are asked to process an ever-increasing volume of data;

pressure is increased. All this necessitates pipe-like function, because there simply is not time to ponder deeply the enormous amount of data fed to us. By necessity we remain shallow, never realizing until our seams break or until the pressure is off how hollow and used we feel.

David and his Psalms teach that we will have pressures. But the lesson which is shared is that we should be like reservoirs, not pipes. We need to be selective in the sources from which we draw, to take time to stay in touch with our feelings, and to exercise our spiritual strength. We need to contribute out of fullness rather than function only to pass on what comes to us without assimilating its value.

I find it striking that the twenty-second Psalm, expressing the pain of pressure, is followed by the famous twenty-third which talks about life as a reservoir. The image is life as a cup which overflows! The images of that passage quiet the pipe-like soul!

God makes me lie down in *green* pastures. He leads me beside *still* waters. Even under the ultimate pressure of the fear of dying I shall sense his strength and protection. I am not alone. There is a banquet table before me. My life overflows! All of these images express the value of seeking the calm settings and moments. To lie down in a green field or to walk by still water makes us receptive to the small voice which quietly restores our sense of belonging and worth.

David was a busy man. But it is obvious that he knew the value of recess. He reflects the peace of one who intentionally took time to stay in touch with God and himself as a son. David was busy and harried, but he also lay alone in green pastures and felt the warm sun. Such experience gave him the strength to carry on.

There are pressures to be sure. But taking time to follow where God leads restores the pipelike soul, and fashions us deeper vessels for the inpouring of his sustaining spirit.

12 ∽

Empathy—The Talk of the Town

Once there was a couple who had a son who was mentally ill. The mental illness of this boy was severe. Sometimes, right in the middle of a public place, their son would start doing strange things and making strange noises. When the family would go to the market, the son would sometimes jump up on a vegetable stand and crow like a rooster. When his father would take him to church the boy would sometimes, right in the middle of the service, jump down on the floor and act like a snake.

Well, the parents loved their son and they tried all kinds of things to help him, but nothing worked. At last, they realized all they could do was what they had always done—accept him as he was and love him.

All would have been fine except for one thing—people talked. The boy was known throughout the town as the "crazy boy." When people would see him with his family they would follow, hoping he would do something strange. Everyone talked about the boy, and some made fun of him. The effect of all this talk was that the boy had no friends. His family tried to protect him from hurt by keeping him home and taking him out only on special holidays or sometimes to church. The boy was the talk of the town, and the talk caused him and his family far more suffering than did his illness.

It was so all the boy's life, until one day he was a grown man and all alone with no place to go but church. There he met a man unlike any he had known before. Listen to what happened.

Coming down to Capernaum, a town in Galilee, he (Jesus) taught the people on the Sabbath, and they were astounded at his teaching, for what he said had the note of authority. Now there was a man in the synagogue possessed by a devil, an unclean spirit. He shrieked at the top of his voice, "What do you want with us, Jesus of Nazareth? Have you come to destroy us? I know who you are—the Holy One of God." Jesus rebuked him: "Be silent," he said, "and come out of him." Then the devil, after throwing the man down in front of the people, left him without doing him any injury. Amazement fell on them all, and they said to one another: "What is there in this man's words? He gives orders to the unclean spirits with authority and power, and out they go." So the news spread, and he was the talk of the whole district (author's paraphrase of Mark 1:21-28).

Can you imagine that scene? Here is a mentally ill person who has been talked about all his life—the talk of the town because he is suffering. And the talk makes him worse. But in one great moment, all that changes. Where once the townspeople talked of an illness, Mark records they now only discuss the person who brought the cure!

Who and what do we talk about? Do we find ourselves talking about the problems and the sufferings of others? Or do we talk about who or what might be the cure?

Many of the problems which people encounter would not be nearly as painful or debilitating to them if others would stop talking *about* them. Most people can accept their failures, errors in conduct, and errors in judgment and make positive changes. What most of us can't face very easily, and what inflicts the lasting injury, are those persons who, for no other reason than for something to do, find great enjoyment in talking *about* the person who has made a mistake.

Such folks are great newscasters. They make the mistake of another person exciting conversational material. But they know little of Christ. Such newscasters care nothing for the cure the hurting folks may need.

Take the office manager at work. Everyone knows he has become an alcoholic. A lot of the office girls snicker about the time he got drunk one afternoon and forgot where he left his car. The guy and his drinking are the talk of the town. Many wait to hear a new story caused by his drinking problem and tell it to a friend. No one cares that the man is forty-two years old and has finally realized that his homelife has been a shambles for three years. No one cares enough to suggest a cure.

Or how about the girl in high school that the guys all talk about in the locker room? She's known as easy and good for experience. The "in" crowd delights in talking about her dates. She's the talk of the town! But no one cares that her father doesn't hug her, that her mother doesn't touch her, and that she hasn't had the interest of their discipline for seven years. She has to feel close to someone, somehow.

The office manager's drinking is a serious problem. The high school girl's promiscuity is a great mistake. But what about the sin of destructive gossip?

Isn't it amazing how we human beings can have such a wonderful gift as speech, yet so often use it to convey such hurtful thoughts or stories about others we may know only by sight? We can be caustic, you and I. We can talk about the activities of others, maliciously gossip about their life-style, the ways they spend their money, their childrearing, or even their clothes! Would we not do better to talk about the hurts of people in terms of who brings the cure, or to *furnish* the cure they need?

The way to begin to accomplish this is to make it a moral commitment never to talk about someone unless we are also willing to talk *with* that person about the life he or she leads and the lives we lead.

The great difference between Jesus and the townfolk who gossiped about the mentally ill man is that *he cared for the man more than he cared for the man's problem.* So often we are only interested in the problems or failures of others and not the person who suffers them. There are people all around us (and we ourselves) who have made mistakes or who suffer from problems of which we are not fully aware. To focus on the mistake or the handicap of another person and then spread the news, caring nothing for the person or his family, is a great wrong. It is a great wrong because in doing the talking, in spreading the news, we are intentionally making someone and related innocent persons the object of ridicule rather than persons of sacred worth.

If you hear that a friend has trouble or has made a mistake, pray for that person and let him or her know you care anyway. Then let us keep our mouths shut.

The Hebrew proverb is right, and in the temple Jesus lived its message:

> Gossip can be sharp as a sword,
> but the tongue of the wise heals.
> Proverbs 12:18

✑ 13

Doubt—If I Had Only
Done Otherwise

I want to introduce to you two very special friends of mine. I want you to read their stories and become caught up for a time in the matrix of their lives. I want you to listen to what they hear, to see what they see, and to feel in your heart what they feel in theirs. Perhaps in them you will see something of yourself, and maybe through them you will hear the voice of Jesus Christ calling out to you where you are and giving meaning to the precious life that is uniquely your own.

Joanie is thirty-seven. She has three children and a reasonably successful husband who is an accounts receivable manager for a manufacturing company. Her children are a great challenge to her. She has an attractive fifteen-going-on-twenty-one-year-old daughter, a thirteen-year-old rude son, and an eight-year-old laundry problem that makes more messes in three minutes than Joanie can "unmess" in four hours.

On many mornings, after the children have gone to school and Joanie's husband has gone to work, Joanie walks into the living room. She goes over to a row of shelves that are on the wall to the right side of the fireplace. On the third shelf from the bottom, and back in a corner, is a special little mahogany box. Joanie reaches up and takes that box from the shelf, walks slowly across the carpet, and sits down on the couch on the other side of the living room.

There she takes that mahogany box, places it in her lap, and then carefully opens the lid. With even greater care, she reaches inside the box and takes out a dried rose and an old ticket stub. She holds them in her hand. As she looks at that rose she not only remembers her past, but becomes very sad about her present life. Joanie remembers when that rose was fresh, and one of twenty-four that were presented to her in front of a cheering and applauding audience that had just watched her play Desdemona in Shakespeare's *Othello* in the college theater. In her mind's ear, she hears the cheers and remembers the sound of the applause. She remembers the time when the director of the play called her aside during rehearsals and said to her in a very sincere manner, "Joanie, you have the talent to be a great actress. You ought to pursue this career."

Joanie remembers her sorority sisters as she looks at that rose, as well as a young man named Mike. Mike was the college tennis star to whom she was once pinned. As she looks at that rose, she remembers all these things and tears stream down her cheeks. She becomes unhappy in her present life as she looks back. As Joanie thinks about all the things that the rose represents, in her mind her husband becomes more and more insensitive to her. She decides that love is gone, because he doesn't even kiss her goodbye in the mornings. The children become a hassle instead of a gift. She sees them as an encumbrance and a continual demand upon her time. Joanie's life becomes confused as she looks at the rose, until she finally bursts with rage and screams, "I'm thirty-seven and I'm wasting my life washing out moldy tennis shoes!"

Soon Joanie carefully puts the rose back in the mahogany box. As she replaces the box on the shelf in the living room, she asks herself over and over again, "What if I had done otherwise? Just think what I could be today."

There's a forty-three-year-old man named Thomas. He is vice-president of manufacturing for a hydraulic hose company. His wife is a registered nurse, and they have two sons. The oldest is a junior in college.

Tom, because of his position, has a very attractive office, and generally when you see him that is where you have to meet. That is really the only place he has been available for many years. There are two large chairs that sit in front of his long, oak-topped desk. It is from behind this desk that Tom looks out at you as you walk into his office. On the wall behind his desk are civic awards, company merit citations, and family photographs. But most special to Tom is a large picture, expensively framed, that hangs on one side wall of his office. It is a picture of his uncle's charter fishing boat on Chesapeake Bay.

By all the signs, Tom is a successful man. But the signs don't tell all the story. Early in the afternoon, when he is alone in his office, Tom opens the top drawer of his desk and takes out a memo that was sent to him three months ago. As he reads the memo, he glances up at the picture of his uncle's charter fishing boat, and tears fill his eyes. (He's glad he has the door locked because he doesn't want anyone to see him like this.) The memo reads that the company for which he works has been purchased by a large conglomerate, and that there is likely to be a shake-up in management. Tom remembers, as he looks at that picture, how his uncle, twenty-one years before, had asked him to go into business with him on that boat. He remembers his uncle saying, "Tom, we won't make a lot of money, but the life is good. The sea is a hearty life. You will come to love her. You will know your family and have time to raise your sons."

Instead, Tom said no and joined a large company. He traveled a lot. Tom had gone through the company rat race, hoping he would one day be president of the firm. But now, as he reads that memo, he knows it won't be possible. He looks down the road and sees at least twenty more years of horizontal job changes and moves, with the same salary rate and responsibilities. He feels locked in. The pressure is already affecting him physically. And so, as he sits behind the desk on this afternoon and looks at that picture, he asks the question, "What if I had done otherwise? How I wish I were on that boat."

We have all taken a backward look and pondered what our lives would be today had we made decisions other than the ones we have made.

The problem is, it seems to me, that in our society today we're making a profession of looking back. We have nostalgia fads and the golden years, the bygone days that are said to be so glorious. More and more of us are looking back at roads and paths we've taken ten and twenty years earlier. When we look back, we wonder if we've made the right choice. We are looking back and asking the question, "What if I had done otherwise?" to our own detriment and sometimes to our own destruction.

All this has done to us is convince some of us, like Joanie and Tom, that our present lives are terrible because we made a wrong choice ten or twenty years ago. Or it makes others of us feel that each decision we must make today must be made knowing *all* the future variables, so that ten years from now we won't look back and think we made a mistake. Some of us are so frightened about what might happen in the future with the decisions we make now that we wrestle, hesitate, and postpone the decisions facing us.

It doesn't matter which point of view we endorse, the outcome is the same: stalemate, inaction, sadness, and sometimes, chronic depression.

For instance, how many of us know parents, or maybe even are parents, who have children now pretty much on their own? We may not like their life-style. We may wonder how in the world they could act the way they do, when they had the kind of home they had. And so, we look back and say things like, "It's my fault! If I hadn't spanked him so hard," or, "If I had let her single date when she was fifteen," or, "If I had let him buy the car he wanted, maybe things would be different now." Do you know people like that, who look back and become depressed today because they think they made wrong choices in the past?

Several months ago I called my home. Grace was in the laundry room, and so Laura answered the phone. She's pretty much an average three-year-old, and I said, "Laura, what are you doing?" She said, as matter-of-factly as she could, "Kicking baby Wayne." And she was! He was screaming in the background. Well, one day I may regret the tone of voice I took over the phone. Parents should be prepared, I suppose. But usually when we make decisions in our lives, we do so in response to the immediate situation. We don't have time always to take the best action or Dr. Spock's advice, because the only action we want to take is the one to stop the kicking.

Years ago there was a man who spoke to the hearts and minds of people. They loved him because, among other things, he made sense. He looked out over the crowds that he spoke to each day, and he saw people who were miserable in their lives because they were looking back and living in the past. Some were filled with hate because of things that happened months and years back. Some were depressed because they regretted decisions they had made. And some were bitter because their lives hadn't turned out the way they had expected. Jesus looked out at the crowd and said to them all, "If you put your hand to the plow and then you look back, there's no two ways about it, you're just not fit for the Kingdom'' (author's paraphrase of Luke 9:62).

He wasn't being cruel, and he wasn't being intolerant; he was just telling it like it is. He was saying that if we have undertaken a task, we must not keep second guessing it all our lives. We will go crazy! We will miss the life God has given us now, because the Kingdom is always a present-tense affair. If we look to the past, pretty soon we will find out that we are not accepting the life we have today.

Well, we have all put our hands to various plows. For how long can we afford to look back?

Jesus always says that the Kingdom is at hand. It's not in front and it's not behind. It's right here today. The past is over. We must repent if appropriate, and live the life we have today because it is just too precious to waste!

We must accept our lives as they are. Then, if we need to make some positive changes, we must do so. But we cannot make any changes until we accept what we have. Our lives, whether we believe it or not, are part of the Kingdom, and they are brand new gifts to us each day to do with what we will.

How much? How much? Really now, how much do we love Jesus Christ? How much? Do we love him enough that, if we are like Joanie, we could give him the rose? How much do we trust him? Do we trust him enough that if we are like Tom we could give him the picture on the wall? Life in abundance awaits the decisions that we will make.

CONCLUSION

✌ 14

At Lystra Sat a
Crippled Man

At Lystra sat a crippled man, lame from birth, who had never walked in his life. This man listened while Paul was speaking. Paul fixed his eyes on him and saw that he had the faith to be cured, so he said to him in a loud voice, "Stand up straight on your feet"; and he sprang up and started to walk (Acts 14:8-10).

In Paul's day it was not unusual to see people with handicapping conditions. along heavily traveled streets. Lystra was no exception. There, as in other cities and towns, these people were forced to beg for their social security. The financial result of their begging was meager, as the impetus for more fortunate persons to provide assistance for such maimed people was casual at best.

A person with such a condition in the time of Paul was

thought to be affected that way because he or she had offended God. His physical affliction was believed to be a divine punishment. Such a theological perspective led to general public ridicule and abuse of these persons.

The text above records that Paul saw a crippled man in the Asia Minor city of Lystra. The fact of his seeing this crippled person is remembered for two reasons.

It is remembered first because the crippled man himself rejected the view that his maimed legs meant that he was not as good as other people. Acts records this by saying that the man "had the faith to be cured." And the second reason that Paul's seeing this crippled man at the Asia Minor city of Lystra is remembered is that Paul, unlike others, could see past the man's crippled condition to the person he truly was.

While I was going to seminary my wife, Grace, taught school in the city of Durham, North Carolina. In one of her music classes was a little girl named Alisha.

Alisha was a plain-looking little girl with lots of spunk and grit. She, like many other children, was interested in learning and had the usual desire to be liked and to be a part of the group. Sitting at her desk, Alisha looked like any other nine-year-old girl. When she stood up though, she immediately caught everyone's attention. Alisha, you see, stood on artificial legs. She had been born with no legs from the knees down. So Alisha held the attention of all as she would, with great difficulty, walk.

The children in the school were pretty rough on Alisha. They referred to her as "the cripple" and made her the target of cruel jokes and hurtful remarks. She was ridiculed for her wooden legs and teased because she was so slow. She was pitied by a few and shunned by many.

Trying to overcome a handicap such as Alisha's in an environment like that isn't easy. In fact, the more intense the ridicule became, the more often Alisha would fall. The harder she was teased, the more difficult it was for her to walk. But Alisha, like the man at Lystra, had the faith to be cured. She refused to be stereotyped or to quit. She had a dream.

Each year Grace put together a school music festival. One of the great events of that festival was the Maypole Dance. All through the year, the girls in the school looked forward to the opportunity to be maypole dancers. Alisha's dream, like that of many of the other girls in the school, was to dance around the maypole.

Finally the day came when the tryouts for the Maypole Dance were to be held. Girls who, throughout the year, had been interested in and looking forward to the event congregated in the school gymnasium. Much to everyone's surprise, in came Alisha.

At first the other girls were stunned; then many began to laugh and snicker at the thought of Alisha's even attempting to do a maypole dance. But as the tryouts began and as Alisha tried to do the dance, the other children began to see Alisha in a brand new way and to recognize the special faith that she had. As the children watched her, a transformation occurred within them. They, like Saint Paul with the crippled man at Lystra, accepted Alisha for who she was and, for the first time, saw beyond her handicap.

Because of Alisha's faith and because of the children's recognition and acceptance of her, attitudes changed and miracles began to happen. Children who were once cruel became supportive. Because they were supportive and kind, Alisha began to walk better and even learned to jump rope. And then the greatest miracle of all occurred. On the night of the spring festival, Alisha was seen by one and all dancing on artificial legs around the maypole, hand in hand with those who had helped her to walk and given her greater incentive to dance.

Now as in the time of Saint Paul, people too often respond to those with handicapping conditions in unfortunate ways. We resent them because they hinder us. We become angry with them when their problems cause their needs to come before our own. Sometimes we ridicule them, feeling that by putting them down we can avoid them. Or we indulge in great pity for them, conveying the attitude, "I'm okay, you're sick. What's wrong with you?"

One of the reasons we treat these people so, I believe, is that physically crippled persons remind us that we are all crippled to some degree. We all have psychological or physical handicaps that cause us to stumble.

One of the great things about the Christian faith is that it calls together people who are handicapped in many ways to be the church. We come together in the church not to have our handicaps exposed, but out of faith in Christ, so that we can be healed by a God who is revealed in his caring love.

There is not one of us on this earth that is not handicapped in some way, to some degree. Some of us have physical ailments which cause us pain and hinder us from walking effectively. Some of us are affected emotionally because of psychological disorders caused by being hurt or abandoned by others. Some of us are twisted spiritually so that we do not trust God very much and thus find ourselves hampered in the giving of ourselves to others. Each one of us is handicapped to some degree in at least one of these areas. So sometimes when the pressures of stereotypes, false gods, miscast roles and unowned feelings build, we do not walk, but stumble and fall. We all need help. That's one reason why the church is so important, and why it is so important for us to participate in it. It is within the church that we learn that Christ would enable us to walk and run.

There are many things in this life that cripple us. There are the pressures of the work place, the pressures of the home. There are the struggles of being effective parents, the ambiguity of being a young person. And, there is the difficulty of being faithful to God in a pluralistic world.

Because of the crippling effects of society, how-to-cope books line the shelves, tranquilizers are too often used to numb us to reality, and preachers of the "electric church" fill the airwaves with condemnation for sinfulness, while professing that they have the truth that heals.

But we need to know this: we need to know that the basic message of Christian faith is that God sent his Son to make known the *acceptable* year of the Lord. Christ came to let all of us know that no matter what cripples us, we are not

127

relegated to the roadside in order to beg to be noticed. Rather we are greatly loved.

We cannot be cured or heal the crippling forces which affect us or other people by ridiculing, making fun, pitying, being condescending, or by getting angry and condemning what is around us. We can only mend what is broken, heal what is hurt, and warm what is cold by loving enough to learn what the schoolchildren learned about Alisha and what Paul demonstrated at Lystra. That is: because of the love of Christ, we must see through what cripples us and others to the persons we are and they are. That alone can enable us to join hands and dance together in service to a risen Christ who makes us one in the spirit and one in the Lord.